PENGUIN

THE CAPTURED GAZELLE

MUHAMMAD TAHIR GHANI (d. 1669), better known as Ghani Kashmiri, is arguably the greatest Persian poet of Kashmir and one of its literary and cultural icons. Highly popular in India and the larger Persian-speaking world up to the modern times, he influenced many generations of Persian and Urdu poets in India. Ghani's forte lies in his remarkable use of language to create poems with multiple layers of meaning. This, along with his versatility in creating delightful metaphors and images, makes him one of the few medieval poets with a striking appeal to the modern reader.

MUFTI MUDASIR FAROOQI was born and raised in Srinagar. He has published on literary theory, postmodernism and Indo-Persian poetry. He is senior assistant professor in the Department of English, University of Kashmir.

NUSRAT BAZAZ is associate professor in the Department of English, University of Kashmir, where she teaches American poetry and fiction.

THE CAPTURED GAZELLE

The Poems of Ghani Kashmiri

Tahir Ghani

Translated from the Persian by
Mufti Mudasir Farooqi and Nusrat Bazaz

PENGUIN BOOKS

PENGUIN BOOKS
Published by the Penguin Group
Penguin Books India Pvt. Ltd, 11 Community Centre, Panchsheel Park,
New Delhi 110 017, India
Penguin Group (USA) Inc., 375 Hudson Street, New York,
New York 10014, USA
Penguin Group (Canada), 90 Eglinton Avenue East, Suite 700, Toronto,
Ontario, M4P 2Y3, Canada (a division of Pearson Penguin Canada Inc.)
Penguin Books Ltd, 80 Strand, London WC2R 0RL, England
Penguin Ireland, 25 St Stephen's Green, Dublin 2, Ireland
(a division of Penguin Books Ltd)
Penguin Group (Australia), 707 Collins Street, Melbourne, Victoria 3008,
Australia (a division of Pearson Australia Group Pty Ltd)
Penguin Group (NZ), 67 Apollo Drive, Rosedale, Auckland 0632,
New Zealand (a division of Pearson New Zealand Ltd)
Penguin Books (South Africa) (Pty) Ltd, Block D, Rosebank Office Park,
181 Jan Smuts Avenue, Parktown North, Johannesburg 2193, South Africa

Penguin Books Ltd, Registered Offices: 80 Strand, London WC2R 0RL,
England

First published by Penguin Books India 2013

Translation copyright © Mufti Mudasir Farooqi and Nusrat Bazaz 2013
Introduction copyright © Mufti Mudasir Farooqi 2013

All rights reserved

10 9 8 7 6 5 4 3 2 1

ISBN 9780143415626

Typeset in Adobe Caslon Pro by Eleven Arts, New Delhi
Printed at HT Media Limited, Noida

ALWAYS LEARNING   **PEARSON**

Contents

Acknowledgements

Many people have contributed in different ways to make the present work possible. Firstly, I express my immense gratitude to Sunil Sharma of Boston University for his invaluable recommendations, unfailing encouragement and kindness. I am also very grateful to my dear teacher Muhammad Amin who offered to read the introduction and gave valuable suggestions.

I want to express my gratitude to many friends for their support. To my colleagues in the English Department, University of Kashmir, I extend a warm expression of thanks for their love and encouragement over the years. Prashant Keshavmurthy deserves special thanks for his friendship and scintillating ideas on Ghani and many other subjects. Others I wish to thank are Iffat Maqbool, Shadab Arshad, Inayat Rasool, Sajad Darzi, Abir Bazaz, Abid Ahmed, Maroof Shah and, last but not least, Sivapriya and Richa, our editors at Penguin, for their kindness and excellent editing of the manuscript. I also thank all the friends and participants in the Winter School of the Berlin-based programme, Zukunftsphilologie, held in December 2012 at the Centre for the Study of Developing Societies, New Delhi, where I read and discussed some of these translations and found many eagerly waiting to see the book published.

My family's unconditional love has been indispensable throughout. I owe an enormous gratitude to my parents, parents-in-

Acknowledgements

law, my brother, Muzamil, and particularly, to my wife, Huma, and son, Khaleed. It is to them that I dedicate all my efforts that have gone into this work.

I cannot adequately express my gratitude to Nusrat Bazaz for her unswerving generosity. She gladly gave her time to read my translations, suggested revisions and, in the end, allowed me to have the final word on them. Lastly, I must put on record that I alone am responsible for the final draft of this work and its errors or imperfections are solely mine.

Mufti Mudasir Farooqi

A Note on the Translation

Translating poetry is generally understood to be a difficult task. Perhaps the most difficult challenge facing any translator is to render in translation the subtleties and multivalence of the original which the poet has deliberately cultivated and which account for its richness and beauty. In the strict sense, translating poetry may be well-nigh impossible but it is nonetheless necessary. Once, arguing in favour of the possibility of translation, Goethe had remarked that the essence of poetry lies in that which is preserved when it is translated into prose. Formal properties such as rhyme and rhythm are undoubtedly a great part of the pleasure that poetry provides, but the element by which poetry becomes poetry first and foremost—and which is definitely translatable—is the image or metaphor.

Ghani strikes us as a master craftsman of the poetic image. The translators have, therefore, tried to remain as faithful as possible to the content and imagery of the original. At the same time, they have also been fully aware that the worst sin in translating poetry is dullness. Steering a middle course between an overly literal and a very free rendering has thus been the guiding principle in this work.

A word also needs to be said about the selections made from the available corpus of Ghani's poetry. Here the aim has been to present before the readers what, in the view of the translators, is the best in Ghani. Consequently, only a few ghazals have been translated in full, a decision taken due to their conviction that each *sher*, or verse, in a ghazal is a small poem, a self-contained unit of meaning related to other verses only by virtue of the formal features of metre and rhyme. So, omitting one or more verses from a ghazal in no way hampers the enjoyment of others. Besides this, leaving out some verses has sometimes been due to the fact that they simply defy any adequate translation.

A noticeable aspect of Ghani's *divan*, or collection, is an unusually large number of solitary verses. The present work, therefore, features a good number of them. In addition to these, some *rubaa'iyaat*, or quatrains, and one of the two *masnavi*s describing Kashmir's winter have also been included. A *masnavi* is a narrative poem of indefinite length written in internally rhyming lines. The verses in this volume follow the same sequence as the Persian *divan*.

The transliteration of the original Persian, on the facing pages, is not a standard one, but will certainly help those who can read Persian and also those who wish to get the feel of the original on the phonetic level.

A Note on the Transliteration

The apostrophe (') has been used for *hamza* as in shitā'iyah and the opening quotation mark (‘) has been deployed for *ain* as in rubā‘iyāt. The diacritical mark of a bar above vowels indicates long vowels, such as in zabān for zabaan, khushkī for khushkee and ṭūfān for toofaan. Different symbols have been used for different letters with similar but non-identical sounds in the Persian alphabet, as below.

t	for *tey* as in tangī	z	for *zey* as in zāhid
ṭ	for *toi* as in ṭabīb	ẑ	for *zaud* as in maẑbūt
ṣ	for *sey* as in ṣamar	ź	for *zoi* as in źāhir
s	for *seen* as in sāmān	gh	for *ghain* as in Ghanī
ś	for *saud* as in śaid	g	for *gaaf* as in magar
ĥ	or *hai* as in ĥalqah	q	for *qaaf* as in qālīn
h	for *hey* as in hamīshah	k	for *keef* as in kitāb
kh	for *khai* as in kharāb	j	for *jeem* as in junūn
ż	for *zaal* as in ma‘żur	ĵ	for *zhey* as in miĵgān

Introduction

Ghani: Life and Reception

Mulla Muhammad Tahir Ghani, popularly known as Ghani Kashmiri, is one of the foremost poets of the Persian language in the Indian subcontinent and probably the most popular of all the Persian poets of Kashmir. Although many aspects of Ghani's life remain obscure and sources differ concerning the year of his birth, it may be said that he was born sometime in the early seventeenth century, probably in the first decade, in the old city of Srinagar, and lived mostly as a recluse, never attending any royal court in Kashmir or elsewhere. He belonged to a well-known Ashai family in Srinagar, who were immigrants from Central Asia. Nothing else is known of his family. Historians agree that Ghani was a pupil of an eminent scholar and poet of his day, Mulla Mohsin Fani. The epithet Mulla, which also goes with Ghani, suggests that he must have received traditional religious education in a local school and also achieved distinction as a scholar. How he earned his living is not known, although his aversion to making poetry a means for it is well known, a trait especially remarkable in an age when it was customary for poets to employ their poetic skills to seek favours from rulers and nobles.

Not only did Ghani abhor attending court, he also strikes us as a man living an extremely frugal and ascetic life, confining himself to a solitary corner of his humble abode, silently watching over the dismal condition of his people and, occasionally, though obliquely, alluding to it in his poetry. Unassuming by any standards, he yet seems highly conscious of the quality of his verse and sometimes expresses satisfaction over the fame his verse earned him:

> My verses have travelled to Iran.
> No, not just Iran, they have
> travelled the world.
>
> My name has attained
> such fame in India,
> As the signet ring's mark
> in black ink.*

That these assertions, while being part of the accepted tradition of *fakhr*, or boasting of one's poetic prowess, also carry some historical validity is borne out by the testimonies of several biographers and literary historians. One of the earliest chroniclers, Sirajuddin Ali Khan Arzoo (1689–1756), gives the following estimate of the poet in his *Majma'un Nafaa'is*:

> There are few poets comparable to Ghani among the latter-day poets not only in Kashmir but also the rest of India. He excels not only his contemporaries but also most of his predecessors in his ability to compose novel poetic meanings, and commands a great felicity of expression.[1]

---

* All translations in the introduction are by the translators of this volume, except where indicated.

And the celebrated modern critic Shamsur Rahman Faruqi approvingly quotes another *tazkirah* writer:[2]

> Ghani Kashmiri, a poet who commanded respect and admiration from Indians and Iranians alike, and about whom Ikhlas says, 'To this day, there hasn't been a *mazmun* composing poet like him from that heart-pleasing territory [Kashmir], and in fact none like him has come out of the whole of India.'[3]

Ghani's fame during his lifetime is all the more remarkable because the Mughal period witnessed an unprecedented surge in literary activity in India, while Kashmir attracted some of the outstanding talent in Persian from India and Iran. At a time when India had become a 'garden of nightingales', it required an exceptional poetic talent to gain distinction. Some of the eminent Iranian poets who visited Kashmir during Ghani's lifetime include Sa'ib Tabrizi (d. 1677 or 1678), Abu Talib Kalim Kashani (d. 1651), Muhammad Quli Salim Tehrani (d. 1647 or 1648), Muhammad Jan Qudsi Mashhadi (d. 1646 or 1647) and Mir Ilahi (d. 1654). In fact, there is evidence that he forged lasting friendships with many of them and his *divan* contains a short elegiac chronogram written on the death of Abu Talib Kalim, Shah Jahan's poet laureate:

Alas, from the confines
of this garden has flown
Talib, that nightingale,
to the garden of bounty.

He has left, dropping the pen
from his hand.
Kalim has traversed this path
without his staff.[4]

Why doesn't the pen shed
tears of sorrow,
For poetry is orphaned
by the death of Talib?

Pining for him, the hearts
of poets,
Like the tongues of their pens
are cleft in two.

Yearning for him for ages
under the earth,
Qudsi and Salim have thrown
dust over their heads.

At last, their longing
finds fulfilment
And all three are
together united.

Ghani proclaims the date
of his death:
'Due to Kalim the Tur
of meaning was radiant.'[5]

Among the many stories popular about Ghani and also reported
by some historians is the one that describes his meeting with Sa'ib,
the famous Iranian poet who visited Kashmir with his patron and the
then Mughal governor of the Valley, Zafar Khan Ahsan, himself a
poet of repute. Having failed to understand the meaning of *kraal pan*,
which in Kashmiri means the potter's thread and which Ghani had
used in one of his verses, Sa'ib had decided to meet him personally. He
was highly impressed to meet someone whose verses bore a marked
resemblance to his own. The verse reads:

muye mayaan-e tu shudah kraal pan
kard judaa kaasaye sar haa zi tan

Your hair-thin waist has
become the potter's thread,
Severing off from bodies
many a head.

It was, however, this verse that delighted him the most:

husn-e sabz-e bakhat-e sabz maraa kard aseer
daam hamrang-e zamin bud giriftaar shudam

Splendid down set against a
splendid face had me trapped.
The snare matched the ground
and I was captured.

According to the *tazkirah*s *Majma'un*, *Nafaa'is* and *Majma'ul Fusaha*, Sa'ib was so fond of Ghani's verses that he would often ask people visiting Iran from India what gift they had brought him, meaning, of course, some verses of Ghani. He is said to have copied many of Ghani's verses into his own notebook and, according to Shibli Naumani, also wrote a 'response-ghazal' to him which begins with:

Sa'ib, this ghazal is in response
to the one said by Ghani.
Oh, for those days when my desire's pot
was covered with a lid![6]

Ghani most probably lived his entire life in Kashmir and a rare journey to the Indian plains seems to have ill agreed with his temperament:

The scorching winds of India distress me.
O Fate, take me to the garden of Kashmir.
The heat of exile robs me of peace.
Grant me a glimpse of my land's milky dawn.

Almost all *tazkirah* writers have reported that Ghani adopted an austere lifestyle, shunning the glamour of the world and embracing the Sufi ideal of *faqr*, or poverty. These traits of the poet would be celebrated nearly three centuries later by one of his ardent admirers, Iqbal. In his *Payaam-e Mashriq* (Message of the East) Iqbal sang thus of Ghani:

Ghani, that melodious nightingale of verse
Whose songs resonated in Kashmir's paradise.

Who kept the door shut while at home
And left it open while away from it.

Someone said, 'O soul-stirring bard,
This act of yours leaves all puzzled.'

How well replied he who had no wealth.
No wealth, except in the realm of meaning.

'What friends see me doing is right.
My house guards nothing of value save me.

'As long as Ghani sits in his house
All his wealth abides in it.

'And when this illuminating candle is away
No abode is more desolate than his.'

Ghani seems to have lived long enough to know the ailments attending old age. His pupil Muslim writes that he had been reduced to a skeleton in his last days. He himself repeatedly refers to some painful and distressing physical ailment. A few verses from a fragment describing it are:

Day and night the pain of limbs
keeps me writhing on the floor.
My frame has become one with
the cracks in the mat.

So infirm am I that my stick
too cannot help me stand.
Like a footprint I fail to
rise from the ground.

If my frame continues
to dry up like this,
Soon will my toes look
like shrivelled thorns.

On the heavens I would
take revenge for this affliction,
Only if my hands and feet could
soar high like my thoughts.

The story of your pain
is interminable, Ghani.
How long will you repeat
your tale to the doctors?

And a quatrain reads:

Afflicted with a pain that wears me out,
Would that my life were cut short!

Not fatal, yet this gnawing pain
Will keep me company till my death.

Ghani died in Srinagar in 1669 and lies buried in a grave near his
home, which is now dilapidated. Nasrabadi, a *tazkirah* writer, narrates
the following story about his death:

According to an authentic report, the Emperor of India [that is,
Aurangzeb] wrote to Saif Khan, Kashmir's governor at the time, to
send Ghani to his court. Saif Khan summoned Ghani informing
him of the Emperor's wish. Ghani refused to comply saying, 'Tell
the King that Ghani is insane.' Saif Khan said, 'How can I call
a sane man insane?' At this Ghani tore his shirt and went away
like a frenzied man. After three days he died.[7]

Whatever the truth of the story, it speaks of the reputation that
Ghani enjoyed throughout—a man deeply committed to his land
and wary of the pitfalls of life at court. On his death, Muslim, who
also compiled and edited his *divan*, wrote two chronograms, one of
which is bilingual, consisting of verses with one hemistich in Persian
and the other in Arabic. In the translation below, the italicized lines
indicate the Arabic:

On Ghani's death the young and the old grieve
And all have retired for mourning.
If they ask you of the date of his death, say
'The treasure of talent is hidden beneath the earth.'

And:

Yesterday I heard someone say, 'Ghani is dead.'
'Be silent,' said I. 'You have lost your head.'

Whose hearts are living die not, O ignorant one.
How can he die who lives free of sin?

His death means nothing but a change of realms.
He was pious, pure and bright.

Friends of God live life of a different kind.
He is dead but only to those who cannot see.

When the heart asked the head, 'When did he die?'
It said, 'Say, he didn't live but as Ghani.'[8]

In the last couplet there is a pun on the word 'Ghani', which literally means 'self-contented'. The last couplets of both chronograms give the year 1079 of the Muslim calendar, corresponding to 1669 CE.

Some historians have expressed the opinion that Ghani destroyed a considerable portion of his poetry, a view that does not seem to be true. It is now generally accepted that Muslim brought together his scattered verses and compiled them in a *divan* just a year after the poet's death; the preface written by Muslim to the *divan* suggests this clearly. Ghani has been one of those much-read poets whose *divan* has gone through several editions and has been published in different publishing centres of India at least eleven times. Although there are considerable variations among the different manuscripts of his *divan*, scholars have done commendable work in identifying and compiling the authentic version. The *divan*, published by the Jammu and Kashmir Academy of Arts, Culture and Languages in 1964 and reprinted in 1984, is now accepted as authentic by common consent.

*

Ghani is essentially a poet of the ghazal, although he also wrote a couple of short *masnavi*s, one describing the winter in Kashmir and another satirizing a barber. In addition to these there are ninety-odd *rubaa'iyaat*, or quatrains; a few *qit'aat*, or fragments, describing his physical pain and ailment, and the harshness of winter; and a few chronograms written on the deaths of the poets Abu Talib Kalim and Mir Ilahi, and the Mughal governor Amir'ul Islam Khan. A noticeable thing in his *divan* is the unusually large number of solitary verses and also two- and three-verse poems, which might have originally been part of full-length ghazals.

The only available piece of prose written by the poet himself relates to the incident when he was either actually, or apprehended that he could be, accused of *sariqa*, or plagiarism. The real or possible allegation that Ghani had stolen a verse from Abdul Qadir Badayuni's history and presented it as his own left him distraught. Whatever little can be considered historically valid about Ghani reveals him to be a man equally self-respecting and sensitive. The prose passage shows that he was so distressed by the accusation that he actually gave up writing poetry until he had proved his innocence. He writes:

> God alone is witness to my distressed state. From that day I have held my tongue between under my teeth, not allowing it to utter anything and become a living example of this verse:

> Give up speech to escape
> the stings of critics.
> Sealing one's lips is better
> than composing poetry.

> If you can enjoy a sojourn in the garden of silence like a rosebud, it is senseless to tread the thorn-strewn path of eloquence:

The thornless rose of the garden
of silence is worth picking.
Lay off the prattling tongue
like an unruly slave.

Finally, it was discovered that the original text of Badayuni contained no such verse and a scribe had interpolated one of Ghani's verses into a copy. In fact, while Ghani was extremely sensitive about the charges of stealing poetic themes from other poets, he was also keenly aware that his themes were stolen by others. In a rare and rather uncharacteristic outburst of spite, he heaps scorn on Tughra Mashhadi, a poet notorious for charging others of stealing his poems:

Tughra, whose soul is as base as his body,
the jealous enemy of all pure-hearted men,
complains that poets steal his poems.
They hate to utter his name, let alone his poems.

But he laments that his own verses are stolen:

Friends took my verses.
Pity, they took not my name.

And against those who are wont to steal he asserts his superiority:

From no one do I borrow
the theme of my poetry.
For a delicate disposition
others' speech is a burden.

Moreover, all plagiarists betray their true worth in the very act of stealing:

The poet whose nature
inclines to stealing
Remains obtuse to the novel
meaning he steals.

Ghani is a keenly self-conscious poet who, not unlike other sensitive poets, expects people to recognize his worth, and finding them indifferent he sometimes complains and sometimes pins his hope on posthumous fame:

Fame eluded my verse till the soul
was the body's prisoner.
The fragrant musk found release
once the deer was slain.

Almost all good poets have made the experience of poetic creation or process itself a subject of their poetry and Ghani is no exception. Although he claims absolute mastery in making even intractable themes amenable, he is also aware of the challenge of consistently creating novel and fresh meanings:

Meaning cannot refuse
submission to Ghani's genius.
Poetic themes were fashioned
for him at the dawn of creation.

Every moment it seeks to slip
from the mind's nook.
Fresh poetic meaning is a gazelle
to be captured.

Ghani is aware that mere labour without skill does not make a poet:

However hard the pen might strive,
it fails to attain meaning.
Mere labour without skill
is of no avail.

And yet, any genuine poet has to reflect deeply to produce artistically consummate verse:

Until reflection has made the verse
fit for composition,
Like the pen, my head remains
sunk in my shirt's collar.

Despite his brilliance as a poet, not everything he wrote is excellent. Scholars tend to agree that even the greatest poets have found it difficult to consistently produce the best. In the case of the ghazal, it is not uncommon to come across some very remarkable verses with a few quite ordinary ones in the same ghazal. Ghani himself admits to a certain inability to produce uniformly majestic verse:

Exquisite verse too has
its ups and downs.
Fingers of the shining hand
too vary in length.

The style in which Ghani and most of his contemporaries wrote fell into disfavour in Iran and India in the eighteenth and nineteenth centuries. Consequently, his reputation suffered. The blanket condemnation, or at least disapproval, of this style is mainly responsible for the fact that in Iran, and even in India, Ghani is not known as much today as he was once. But in Kashmir, he has always been looked upon as a poet of remarkable excellence. And despite the waning of Persian language and literature since the past century or so, Ghani has always been held in high esteem both in the popular imagination and among the diminishing class of students of Persian who can read and understand him. In fact, he seems to be one of the very few Persian poets who are still alive in the popular imagination of Kashmiris, the numerous monuments named after him being a proof of this. Not many people know, however, that his genius has been acknowledged by some great poets, including Iqbal and the great Urdu poet Mir Taqi Mir, who found in him a model to be emulated:

kuch gadaa shaa'ir nahin hun Mir mein
tha mera sar-e mashq divan-e Ghani.

Mir, I am a poet of no mean credentials.
For I have honed my skills on the divan of Ghani.

For Iqbal, Ghani was not only a model of Islamic austerity, or *faqr*, but also 'wealthy in the realm of meaning', an admiration borne out by the fact that he used some of Ghani's verses in his poems as *tazmin*, a practice where a poet quotes verses of another poet in his own work. Even some of Ghalib's verses have been found to bear an unmistakable mark of Ghani, which has led some to believe that he used Ghani's verses without acknowledging his indebtedness to him. To substantiate this argument, the following Urdu verse by Ghalib is often quoted:

zabaan-e ahl-e zabaan mein hai marg khaamushi
yeh baat bazm mein roshan hui zabaan-e shama

'Silence means death for men of eloquence.'
In the assembly the candle thus spoke to me.

The verse, as is evident, is almost an exact translation of one of Ghani's:

shud raushanam az sham' ki dar bazm-e hareefan
khaamush shudan marg buvad ahl-e zabaan raa.

'In the assembly of rivals silence means death.'
The burning candle spoke thus to me.

It is almost impossible to say whether it is a case of *sariqa*, plagiarism, or *tavaarud*, unintentional coincidence, although, given the great stature that Ghalib enjoys, most people would be disinclined to call it the former.

Whether or not Ghalib used Ghani's verses, the fact that Mir, whom Ghalib considered the greatest poet of the Urdu ghazal, claims to be no ordinary poet because he has meticulously tried to emulate Ghani is itself a glorious tribute to Ghani. Coincidental as it may again appear, the words Ghalib used for Mir in one of his much-quoted verses were used more than a hundred years before him by a Kashmiri Persian poet Saati (d. 1731) for Ghani. Ghalib's verse:

rekhte ke tum hi ustaad nahin ho Ghalib
kehte hain agle zamaane mein koi Mir bhi tha

Ghalib! You alone are not
a master of Urdu.
They say there was another in the past
by the name of Mir.

seems to be almost an exact Urdu rendition of Saati's Persian verse:

nukta pardaaz agar hast faqir hast imruz
pish azin ahd shunidam ki Ghani ham budast.

If there is a master craftsman
today, it is me.
They say there was another
by the name of Ghani in olden days.

In Kashmir, Ghani has been eulogized by poet after poet—
Mehjoor, Abdul Ahad Azad and Rahman Rahi, to name a few. It is
unfortunate that today the barrier of language makes him inaccessible
to the vast majority of his people.

Persian in Kashmir: An Overview

Among several centres of Persian learning that emerged in the Indian
subcontinent following the establishment of Muslim rule, Kashmir
enjoyed a distinct position. Kashmir's cultural ties with Persia, as
some archaeological findings suggest, date back to ancient times.
But it is with the beginning of the Muslim rule in the fourteenth
century that Kashmir became a great centre of Persian scholarship,
creating a fertile ground for the growth of native writers and attracting
distinguished men from Iran and the rest of India. P.N.K. Bamzai
notes the transition from Sanskrit to Persian thus:

With the increasing patronage extended to Persian scholarship
by the Sultans, Sanskrit receded to the background and Kashmiri
students switched over to the study of Persian, which became
the language of educated classes and even found its way into
the villages. The process was completed with the replacement
of Sanskrit by Persian as the court language during the reign of
Zain-ul-abidin. Thenceforth, Kashmir produced poets and writers
in Persian whose beauty of style and depth of thought equalled
that of the litterateurs of Persia.[9]

Because of its strong cultural, religious, literary and even climatic affinities with Iran, Kashmir came to be known as Iran-e-Saghir (Minor Iran). During Sultan Zain-ul-Abidin's rule (1420–70) Persian received an unprecedented impetus. Himself a poet and a great patron of learning, he is credited with establishing a *daar-u-tarjama*, or a translation bureau, where scholars translated texts from Sanskrit and other languages into Persian and from Arabic and Persian into Sanskrit and Kashmiri. It was here that the Hindu scriptures such as the Ramayana and the Mahabharata were translated into Persian for the first time. Mulla Ahmad Kashmiri, Zain-ul-Abidin's poet laureate and an outstanding scholar, translated the famous Sanskrit works *Rajatarangini* and *Katha Sarita Sagar* into Persian. Under the sultan's patronage, Kashmir's fame as an outstanding centre of learning spread to Iran and Central Asia. For the first time Kashmiri poets started using Persian as the medium of poetic expression and interacting on a regular basis with the poets of Iran.

Persian became the official language in the courts of Shahmiri sultans and also gained immense importance with the arrival of Sufis and preachers from Persia and Central Asia, who poured into the Valley to disseminate the new faith. Persian thus found the opportunity to flourish in Kashmir, with all the sultans, without exception, patronizing it with enthusiasm. Direct contact with Persia and Central Asia gave a further boost to its progress. The most important figure, and according to many the founding father of Muslim Kashmir, was Mir Sayyid Ali Hamadani, the famous Sufi saint and great missionary who left behind a legacy and, in the words of Iqbal, laid the foundations for this Iran-e Saghir. Accompanied by a large number of preachers and scholars, he not only put Islam on a firm footing in Kashmir but also transformed the social, political and economic scenarios of the Valley. He is also believed to have introduced new arts and crafts of Persian or Central Asian origin.

In the religious sphere, perhaps the most significant development in this period was the growth of an indigenous religious movement called the Rishi movement, which, because of its impact, has become an area of great interest for scholars. According to some, the movement, beginning sometime in the fifteenth century and lasting for longer than three centuries, was responsible for bringing the vast majority of Kashmir's population within the fold of Islam. Founded by the well-known saint Sheikh Nooruddin Rishi, it derived its strength from the ideals of *faqr*, or extreme austerity, devotion to the spiritual rather than the formal features of religion and a deep commitment to non-violence. Stressing the inner or esoteric dimension of Islam, the Rishis shunned all ritualism and urged people to live a pure and simple life.

Sheikh Nooruddin was an ardent preacher as well as a poet who wrote didactic verses that had a tremendous appeal among the common people. He also vehemently attacked the decadent religious and social institutions of his day and highlighted the significance of pious living. His untiring appeals to his fellowmen to cultivate the virtues of self-realization, prayer, penance and poverty left an indelible imprint on the collective consciousness of Kashmiris. Nooruddin wrote verses known as *shruk* in Kashmiri, which is probably a derivation from the Sanskrit *shloka*. Nooruddin's poetry has been credited not only for its reformative intent and impact but also for its artistic quality. Furthermore, it has immense historical value as it truly reflects the social reality of its times.

If Nooruddin represents the ascetic and highly disciplined approach of a Muslim Rishi, his elder contemporary, the much-celebrated Lalla, represents a profoundly mystical dimension of Kashmiri consciousness. This Saivite wanderer, whose songs reverberated in almost every Kashmiri household, extolled in her verses mystical ideas of divine love and also attacked all forms of dogmatism and ritualism. Lalla's songs are undoubtedly among the finest specimens of Kashmiri mystical poetry. She is also uniquely fortunate to have found quite a few translators and interpreters, and as a result her poetry is known to many outside Kashmir as well. Her verses, known as *vaakh*s, are quatrains with a specific rhyme scheme and were orally transmitted for a long time. Lalla's thought, enshrined in her *vaakh*s, has had a strong influence on the socio-cultural ethos of Kashmir. One of her *vaakh*s, translated by P.K. Parimoo, is:

> When my mind was cleansed of impurities,
> Like a mirror of its dust and dirt,
> I recognized the self in me:
> When I saw Him dwelling in me,
> I realized that He was everything
> And I was nothing.[10]

The similarities between Lalla and Sheikh Nooruddin have long been a subject of interest for scholars, but what strikes one instantly about both is the ardent mystical passion coupled with the zeal to reform. Deeply mystical and didactic at the same time, their poetry is duly credited with having decisively shaped the literary milieu of Kashmir.

Both Lalla and Sheikh Nooruddin wrote in the vernacular. It is interesting to see how deeply Kashmiri was influenced by Persian during the subsequent centuries. One of the most remarkable instances of how one language can influence another is of Persian's influence on Kashmiri. In fact, present-day Kashmiri owes its existence largely to this influence as most of the Sanskrit words were slowly replaced by Persian ones. Not only did Persian provide a new vocabulary, idioms and phrases to Kashmiri, it also changed generic modes of literary expression, largely substituting earlier forms such as the *vaakh* and *shruk* for the ghazal, *masnavi*, *rubaa'i* and others. Eighteenth- and nineteenth-century Kashmiri poets such as Mahmud Gami and Rasul Mir are known to be the pioneers of the ghazal and *masnavi* in Kashmiri.

It is therefore not surprising that on its arrival in the fifteenth century, Persian poetry found an extremely favourable environment in Kashmir which already had a strong mystical and religious tradition. As G.L. Tikku comments:

> Both the tradition of mystical poetry and of court poetry as they had hitherto developed in Persia arrived in Kashmir in the fourteenth century. And since the carriers of Islam to the valley were more of the mystical than the courtly tradition the first exposure of Kashmiris to Persian literature was dominated by its mystical strain.[11]

The Sufi/Rishi thought also deeply coloured the intellectual and emotional make-up of most of the poets and provided them with a rich repertoire of themes and images to work with. The pervasive influence of Sufi ideas can be gauged from the fact that one hardly comes across a poet who remained immune from it. As we shall see, Ghani's poetry, although not mystical in the real sense, bears a clear imprint of Sufi ideas.

One of the earliest Persian poets was Sayyid Muhammad Amin Uwaisi (d. 1484), the adopted son of Sultan Zain-ul-Abidin and a venerated saint of Kashmir. According to popular narratives, he was assassinated in his own house and wrote the following two quatrains in his own blood on the walls of his house:

> I wander the world,
> a reveller blessed with Messiah's breath
> I don't consider the two worlds worth a fig.
> If my head rolls in your love, I don't care.
> Your secret shall remain hidden in my heart.

No use to me is the worldly wisdom of men.
Make no mistake that guiltless I am slain.
Come now and sing a doleful song on my grave,
That the tyrants' faces be blackened with disgrace.

His poetry marks the beginning of a genuinely Kashmiri contribution to Persian poetry and also lays down the road map for later poets in terms of mood, themes and imagery.

At the end of the Shahmiri rule, the Chaks came to power in 1561 and ruled for a brief period. The Chak rule witnessed a lot of political unrest in Kashmir, which finally led to its annexation by the Mughals in 1586. During the Chak period various genres of Persian poetry were adopted by Kashmiri poets, especially the *masnavi*. The foremost poet of this period is Sheikh Yaqub Sarfi (1529–94), a versatile genius, extremely well schooled in several sciences such as theology, jurisprudence, grammar, mysticism, rhetoric, Quranic hermeneutics and poetry. Sarfi travelled widely and is said to have received guidance from the great masters of mysticism. In Kashmir, he is also known as Jami-e Sani, Jami the Second, after the famous Abdur-Rahman Jami. Sarfi was a prolific writer and as a poet he is known for his excellent quintet of *masnavi*s, a *khamsa*, written in imitation of the famous classical Persian poet Nizami.

Another poet of renown of this period was Habibullah Naushehri or Hubbi (1556–1617), whose lyrics resonate in Kashmir even today. Hubbi wrote poetry in both Persian and Kashmiri and achieved distinction as a Sufi. His poetry is of the devotional kind and is informed by the common Sufi themes of divine love, devotion to one's spiritual mentor, renunciation of the world and the like. In fact, these themes recur in almost all Persian poetry of the period and one hardly comes across any major poet who was also not a Sufi of some kind. A Persian ghazal by Hubbi contains the following beautiful verses:

Say, O heart, why
this difference of creeds?
Why is this one an infidel and
the other a believer?

The Almighty did not create
the difference of sects.
Neither belief nor disbelief, neither
doubt nor faith, have a place there.

My heart is drunk with the cup of
'Am I not your Lord?'[12]
Having come here drunk,
I have no truck with reason or sobriety.

O counsellor! Don't ask me
to give up wine.
My vows to be a drunkard
go back to eternity.

With the wine of Divine Oneness,
the server has filled my cup.
No wonder I have become a cup,
passing from hand to hand.

As the door of our tavern was not
opened to everyone,
The multitudes are astray,
wandering from door to door.

And all who found their way
to the tavern, forthwith
Deserted their homes and came
to sit at its door.

It is noteworthy that many of the poets were also active as preachers, theologians or practising Sufis in some order. Baba Dawood Khaki (d. 1586), to take one example, was a poet, but, more importantly, also a scholar and a Sufi actively engaged in the social and political affairs of his times.

Perhaps the most popular poetic voice of the Chak period was that of Habba Khatun's (d. 1600?), the queen of the last king of Kashmir, Yusuf Shah Chak. Their love story, immortalized in folk songs and even movies, tells how Habba Khatun was living a life of misery as the wife of an ordinary villager when the king, during a hunting expedition, saw her singing and instantly fell in love with her. Their happiness as a married couple proved to be short-lived as Yusuf Shah, invited by Akbar in 1586, was treacherously incarcerated in Patna. Thereafter, Habba Khatun, separated from her lover, sang sad but melodious songs of longing in Kashmiri, which are still extremely popular. A poignant mood of separation informs these lyrics and they also have a striking spontaneity about them:

> What rival of mine has lured
> you away from me?
> Why have you turned
> away from me, my love?
>
> Even at midnight I kept
> my door open for you.
> Didn't you have a moment
> to spare for me?
>
> I am like the fast-melting snow
> in the summer's sun.
> And like a forlorn jasmine
> in the midst of the garden.

Come, for the garden that is yours
yearns for you.
Why have you turned
away from me, my love?

Ceaselessly tears flow
from my eyes.
Desire for you has filled
my whole being.

Why have you forgotten my path?
Why have you turned away from me,
my love?

But it was with the beginning of the Mughal rule in Kashmir that Persian reached its zenith. The fame of Mughal patronage for arts and learning had already spread far and wide, attracting poets and scholars from Persia, making India the most cherished and sought-after destination. Abdul Qadir Badayuni, the noted historian of Akbar's period, in his *Muntakhab'ut Tawarikh* provides an exhaustive list of the poets who attended Akbar's court and received huge rewards for their craft. Literary historians tend to agree that it was the enormous wealth of India that was primarily responsible for the large number of poets pouring in from Iran and elsewhere. Muhammad Quli Salim, one of the Iranian poets who made India his home and died in Kashmir, wrote:

There is no provision for attaining
perfection on the soil of Iran.
Until you turn to India,
the henna fails to bloom.

Kalim Kashani, Shah Jahan's poet laureate, on having to leave India against his will once, lamented:

I am a captive of India and
deeply anguished at this departure.
Where will the fluttering wings take
the bird wallowing in its blood?

Urged by his friends, Kalim
sets off to Iran wailing.
Like the camel bell which journeys
on the feet of others.

Desire for India makes my
wistful eyes turn back.
Though facing forward, I see not
what comes my way.

Even Sa'ib, who stayed in India for a few years, pays his homage in this verse:

Why shouldn't I praise India,
for in its black soil
The flame of my fame donned
the robe of excellence.

Such poetic extolling of India makes perfect sense when we remember that many poets, including Salim and Kalim, were weighed in gold by the Mughal emperors and princes. Dara Shukoh is said to have gifted one lakh rupees to the Iranian poet Mirza Razi Danish for this verse:

taak raa sar sabz kun ai abr-e naisaan dar bahaar
qatrae taa may tavaanad shud chira gauhar shavad

Make the vine greener now
in spring, O spring cloud.
If a drop can become wine,
why should it become a pearl?

Given such patronage, it is no surprise that literary activities flourished with an unprecedented vibrancy. As Kashmir's ties with the rest of India strengthened, many poets, finding the Indian climate appallingly inclement, visited and settled in Kashmir. Kashmir's beauty had already become a favourite topic with many of them. To the Indian climate, which many of them described as *jigar khwaar*, or heart-consuming, they found an ideal alternative in Kashmir. On his first visit to Kashmir in 1589, Akbar was accompanied by a host of poets including Faizi and Urfi, both of whom wrote beautiful odes to its scenic beauty. Stunned by the natural scenery of the land and its extremely pleasant climate, Urfi exclaimed:

> Every scorched soul
> that lands in Kashmir,
> Will come to life and fly away
> even if it were a roasted bird.

Besides Urfi, Faizi and Talib Amuli, who had accompanied the Mughal emperors to Kashmir, there were many others who made it their permanent home. According to some *tazkirah* writers, Kalim, Salim, Qudsi and Tughra are buried in a graveyard that was known as *mazaar-e shu'araa* (poets' graveyard) on the banks of the Dal Lake in Srinagar. With the Mughals gaining a firm foothold in the Valley, the native talent too found a new impetus and took to Persian poetry with renewed enthusiasm. The most prominent name to give it an enormous boost was Zafar Khan Ahsan, the Mughal governor of Kashmir who was in charge of the administration from 1633 to 1641, and then from 1643 to 1647. Himself a poet of eminence, he patronized many others, including Sa'ib whom he brought along to Kashmir. Zafar Khan initiated the Persian tradition of *mushaa'ira*, or poetic symposium, in Srinagar, which was attended by both Iranian and Kashmiri poets. If Sa'ib, Kalim, Salim, Mir Ilahi,

Qudsi and Tughra Mashhadi were the Iranian representative voices, Kashmir offered its native talent through Fasihi, Fitrati, Mulla Zehni, Mehdi, Fani, Ghani, Juya, Guya, Auji and others too numerous to name. The interaction between the two resulted in vibrant literary activity in Kashmir. Zafar Khan—whose *takhallus*, or pen name, was Ahsan—and Sa'ib enjoyed a relationship of mutual respect and admiration. Although he boasts of the high quality of his verse, Zafar Khan also credits Sa'ib with pioneering a new style in writing the ghazal, which became the hallmark of the poetry of the period:

> Among my peers if I boast
> of my poetry, Ahsan,
> It is because it is no less
> remarkable than Fighani's.

> From now on Ahsan shall shun
> the style of his peers,
> For the bounty of Sa'ib's genius has
> inspired his fresh expressions.

Zafar Khan, besides leaving behind a *divan*, which includes ghazals and *rubaa'iyaat*, wrote *masnavi*s such as *Masnaviye Kashmir, Jalwaye Naaz* and *Maikhaanaye Raaz*. Here are a few verses written by him on the beauty of the famous Dal Lake:

> A ride in the Dal refreshes
> the heart and soul,
> Making us renew our
> allegiance to the cup.

> Countless gardens bloom
> in its waters,
> As if early spring
> lies hidden in them.

Myriad blossoms make
it the world's envy.
You could become a
water bird in its love.

The ghazal was the favourite genre of poetry in this period, although *masnavi*s and, on occasion, *qasida*s, or panegyrics, were also written. Ghani's teacher and Yaqub Sarfi's disciple, Mulla Mohsin Fani (d. 1671), was a renowned poet of this period. Believed to be closely associated with the Sufi circle of Dara Shukoh, Fani wrote *masnavi*s and ghazals. His four *masnavi*s that have come down to us are *Masdarul-Asraar*, *Naaz-u-Niyaaz*, *Mah-u-Mihr* and *Haft Akhtar*. For a long time Fani was believed to be the author of a famous treatise on religious schools, *Dabistaan-e Mazaahib* (School of Religions), but modern scholarship has tended to reject this view and Fani's reputation now rests on his poetry rather than any prose work. Here are a few verses from one of his ghazals:

Be not enamoured of your
hue and scent like the rose.
Learn to seal your lips
from speech like the bud.

With your dripping sword
I moistened my throat.
With your stream thus
I made my stream flow.

Every heart rent in the grief
you caused stitches its tear
With the needles of eyelashes
and the thread of tears.

Drowned in the sea, yet not a
drop fell to my lot.
Like a bubble I thus
smashed my own flask.

Fani, none attains his
heart's wish here.
Never pledge yourself
to your desire.

And a few more selected randomly from various ghazals read as
follows:

Until I behold the niche of
those twin eyebrows,
My head shall not bow
in the prayer niche.

My lips know nothing of
my grief-stricken heart.
Where is the confidant to
relate my woes about you?

Fani, seeking redress, says this
to her drunken eye,
'Taking my heart away was like
stealing the lamp from the Kaaba.'

From the revels of wine banquet,
you will relish the real taste,
When one night in drunkenness
you bite your own lip.

The seventeenth century in Kashmir was, therefore, evidently
a period when native poets found vast opportunities of interaction

with their Iranian and Indian counterparts, which helped create an exuberant environment for Persian poetry. The two main trends of poetry, the courtly and the mystical, remained dominant, although Sufi poetry took precedence in terms of the sheer corpus produced as also its general popularity among the readers. In actual practice, however, both courtly and mystical poetry employed the same kind of symbolism and imagery. Alongside these two trends, there were poets like Ghani who were neither court poets nor essentially Sufis and who chose poetry as their preferred mode of expression. Hubbi, Baba Dawood Khaki and Mirza Muhammad Akmal Kamil (1645–1719)—famous for his *Bahrul Irfan*, also known as *Masnavi-e Saani, Masnavi the Second*, after Rumi's *Masnavi*—could be said to have belonged to the latter category. Ghani seems to have made use of both the Sufi and court traditions in his poetry. As we shall see, he followed and contributed to the new style that his Iranian and some Indian contemporaries, many of whom were associated with the courts, had pioneered.

Ghani: Style, Imagery and Themes

In literary circles, Ghani is recognized as the most outstanding native poet and the representative of a specific style of Persian poetry of this period in Kashmir. He is essentially a *mazmun aafreen*, a creator of novel poetic themes and meanings. The ability to create fresh metaphors is the hallmark of all good poetry and Ghani possesses a remarkable gift for creating metaphors and similes which draw striking comparisons between apparently dissimilar and disparate situations or objects. His poetry testifies to his imaginative acumen by which he transforms the data of ordinary experience into rich poetical output.

The sixteenth to eighteenth centuries witnessed the flowering of a new style in the Persian ghazal, which came to be known as *sabk-e*

Hindi or the 'Indian style'. Although many scholars have argued that there is nothing specifically Indian about the style, it is well established that it flourished during the Mughal period when a great influx of poets from Iran and other regions took place. Thus Urfi (d. 1591), Naziri (d. 1614), Talib Amuli (d. 1626–27), Abu Talib Kalim, Salim Tehrani and numerous others made India their home and achieved distinction in Indian courts. In addition to these, countless poets of Indian origin made their mark in Persian and earned accolades and admiration from their Iranian counterparts.

For its detractors, Indian-style poetry marks a departure from the earlier, more indigenous and hence 'purer' styles in its excessive reliance on rhetorical devices such as conceit, pun, ambiguity and paradox. Alleging that the poets of this style employed a hypercerebral and convoluted diction, some Iranian critics of the eighteenth and nineteenth centuries held the Indian and Indian-domiciled Iranian poets responsible for turning their backs on the fluent, simple and mellifluous style of the earlier Persian masters. These opinions gained acceptance due to the emergence of a new literary movement in Iran in the eighteenth century known as *adabi baazgasht*, or 'literary revival'. The movement, not unlike most other literary movements, largely defined itself in contradistinction to what it held to be the characteristic features of the earlier period, dominated by the Indian style. Iranian critics such as Azar Beg, Raza Quli Khan and Taqi Bahar wrote disapprovingly of the style, which they rather pejoratively called the Indian style. In India, Shibli Naumani followed his Iranian counterparts by giving an overall negative estimation of this style. Shibli preferred the term *tarz-e taazah*, or 'new style', to *sabk-e Hindi* and regarded with disfavour its intellectual ingenuity. Echoing the Romantic fallacy, which locates the origin of poetry in the intensity of the poet's feelings and evaluates it by its capacity to affect the reader's emotions, he discredited much of Indian-style poetry, holding that it was not suitable for the ghazal, which is essentially a love lyric. To quote S.R. Faruqi, 'Shibli's disapproval of abstraction, complex metaphoricity, ambiguity and high imaginativeness particularly recalls the prevalent Victorian literary bias against these things.'[13] One is also tempted to quote Faruqi's swipe at Shibli, 'given such friends one doesn't need enemies'.[14] Although Shibli criticized what he called the 'new style', he thoroughly discussed Sa'ib and Abu Talib Kalim, especially the former whom he, in a clear instance of what seems no less than a self-contradiction, regarded as one of the most remarkable poets of the seventeenth century. Shibli, however, righty identified two main features he thought were typical of the Indian style: *tamseel*, or exemplification, and *ihaam*, or wordplay.

Ghani, as we have seen, was a contemporary of Kalim, Salim, Qudsi and Sa'ib, all of whom were present in Kashmir at the same time around the middle of the seventeenth century. There is ample historical evidence to suggest that these poets knew and admired each other. Ghani's meeting with Sa'ib has been reported by many *tazkirah* writers, while his elegiac chronograms on Kalim's and Mir Ilahi's death suggest that the poets enjoyed cordial relations. Critical assessment has generally regarded these poets among the finest practitioners of the Indian style and Shibli too, notwithstanding his somewhat adverse judgement, credits them with refining the 'new style'.

After suffering neglect and disapprobation for a long time, the poets of the Indian style are now being reconsidered in both Iran and India, and the tendency to regard them as preoccupied with artificiality and unhealthy intellectualism is also being examined. To take an example, Mirza Abdul Qadir Bedil (1644–1720), of Azimabad, India, a poet whose name has become almost a byword for complexity of style and who, according to many critics, is the foremost representative of the Indian style, has recently earned his due share of acclaim from Iranian critics. Sa'ib too is now widely recognized as one of the most brilliant poets of his age. His use of metaphors, conceits and other sophisticated poetical devices has found appeal with many modern critics. Paul Losensky remarks thus about Sa'ib:

> Sa'eb is best known for his figures of thought. He frequently refers to his *siva-ye taza* or 'fresh style' and boasts of its *mana-ye bigana* (unfamiliar or alien conceit), *mana-ye rangin* (colorful or variegated idea), and *mazmun-e barjasta* (outstanding conceit). This 'poetics of the new' prizes the unexpected turn of thought or startling connection between image and idea.[15]

And about the artistic merits of his use of *tamseel* he writes:

> Sa'eb is particularly renowned for his mastery of a device called *tamsil* or *ersal-e masal*, in which a claim is made in one half of the verse and an exemplum is adduced to support it in the other, as in this opening verse: 'When a man grows old, his greed grows young: sleep grows heavy just before the dawn' (*adami pir chu shud hirs javan migardad / khvab dar waqt-e sahargah geran migardad*). This technique produces a compound metaphor, a miniature allegory.[16]

Long before Losensky, the renowned Orientalist E.G. Browne, in his *A Literary History of Persia*, had expressed his admiration for Sa'ib in unequivocal terms and attributed it to his brilliant use of various poetic devices.[17]

Not only Sa'ib but Kalim too derives his strength from using similes and metaphors in the same manner as Ghani, which quite often results in delightful poetry.

> He who learns the mysteries of existence
> leaves the world forthwith.
> When one has learned one's lessons well,
> one bids farewell to the school.

My skill delivers me not
from my wretched state.
Like the ruin which does not
flourish by the treasure it hides.

Her union with me is like
the wave's fondness for the shore.
Always with me, yet ever
receding from me.

It will be worthwhile to look at some of Ghani's verses as an
illustration of his dexterity in employing these very devices:

Her decked vermilion feet,
his endless prostrations.
What act, for a Hindu,
can excel the worship of fire!

The skies are in motion to
put my ill luck to sleep.
The rocking cradle brings
comfort to the fretful child.

Fleeting beauty is unworthy of love.
The lamp of lightning's flash attracts
no moth.

Like the whirlwind, I am
ever free from bonds.
Abode on back, I have
no worries of settling down.

From the teller of beads a whisper
reaches my ears:

'A hundred hearts lose their
peace to bring solace to one.'

Ghani, like the shadow of the bird
flying in the course of love,
Falling into the dust will not
disrupt my flight.

The company of her tresses
made me famous throughout.
Like the seal's mark which
owes its fame to black ink.

These verses, chosen randomly from different ghazals, are just a few examples of the delightful use of metaphors and similes that characterizes much of Ghani's poetry. As is instantly evident, they bring out a connection between the idea and the image, thereby bringing about a new set of connotations to bear upon the image. They suggest what Wordsworth described as a process of:

observation of affinities
In objects where no brotherhood exists
To passive minds.[18]

Far from reflecting a lack of organic sensibility that would enable a poet to fuse disparate experiences into an artistic unity, presenting an abstract idea in the first hemistich and following it with concrete exemplification in the second creates a fine balance between a direct abstract proposition and its concretization and helps bring a compactly built world of distich, or *sher*, into existence. The striking manner of linking thought with image is a way of startling the reader, and wonder, surprise and revelation have always been accepted as important functions of poetry. The technique also foregrounds an aspect of reality which tends to be overlaid with familiarity and custom. In fact, modern criticism has recognized defamiliarization as the primary aim of all poetry. Paul Losensky rightly comments on the significance of *bigana*, or unfamiliar poetic meanings:

> *Bigana* suggests the Russian formalist concept of 'making it strange' (*ostranenie*), according to which the power of poetry resides in its ability to disrupt our normal perceptions of literature, language, and reality.[19]

In addition to verses where a poetic proof is presented in the second hemistich of an affirmation stated in the first portion of the distich, Ghani also displays a remarkable dexterity in producing verses that are themselves compound or extended metaphors:

With every step the
anklet cries out:
'Beauty, O fair ones,
has her feet in the stirrup.'

To catch your fragrance,
O rosy-cheeked one,
Spring has its feet
blistered due to dew.

Why grieve if wine's
water bird is slow to take off?
In capturing the colour that has fled
it becomes a royal falcon.

I illuminate the world,
myself darkened by ill luck.
How can the lamp rid itself
of its shadow?

Coming out of the beloved's eye
the kohl stick remarked:
'A stroll through the tavern
wipes away the dust of thoughts.'

These and many other such verses testify to Ghani's ability to imagine
situations which are not just embroidered with certain figurative
devices, but where the fundamental imaginative process reveals itself
to be metaphorical. The metaphors used, at least in some verses, reveal
a mode of experiencing the subtle aspects of reality rather than an
embellishment of a prior known fact.

Moreover, fresh poetic meanings can be created from a well-worn
image only by using it in contexts that bring its different connotative
aspects into play. Ghani, working with the conventional repertoire
of images of the Persian ghazal, invests some of them with multiple
and often contradictory meanings. An example of this is the image
of *habaab*, or bubble, which is used to suggest diverse ideas in the
following verses:

Too flimsy to bear ties are
the apparels of the burdenless.
Like an air bubble my robes
are without a stitch.

Though the sea harbours
meanings in plenty,
Mine is a pearl,
theirs a bubble.

The silent lips of the bubble
whispered into the diver's ears:
'A pearl more precious
you shall never find.'

No one fathoms the sea of
nakedness like me.
Like the bubble my skin
and garment are one.

A dull mind may fix its gaze on the book
Yet meaning shall remain beyond its grasp.
The empty-headed fail to fathom the depths,
Like a hollow bubble they can never plunge the sea.

Alas! So swiftly did youth's ebriety pass
Before we could savour fully the ruby wine.
We opened our eyes to behold the world
And the bubble burst . . .

Opening the eye in
love's tempestuous sea
Brought me to naught
like a bubble.

The bubble thus becomes a symbol for such diverse ideas as hollowness, incapacity, lightness, transience, perfection and nakedness.

Among the earlier Persian poets, *ihaam*—that is, double entendre or wordplay—was used by Amir Khusrau to achieve great poetical effects. But in the hands of later poets such as Sa'ib, Kalim and Ghani, the technique was further refined and used with remarkable finesse. As S.R. Faruqi remarks, 'wordplay infuses new life into old themes, expands the horizon of meaning, and often makes for an ambiguity of tone which enriches the total feel of the poem'.[20] A few examples from Ghani's poetry will illustrate how he employs this device to produce what may be called 'multilayered poetry'.

az kinaaram dukhtar-e raz kard taa pahloo tihee
kaar-e man aknoon Ghani baa tifl-e ashk uftaadah ast

Since the daughter of vine
has slipped from my embrace,
Ghani, I am left to deal
with the child of tears.

In this verse the Persian *dukhtar-e raz* in the first hemistich denotes wine but literally means 'daughter of vine'. Likewise, *tifl-e ashk* in the second hemistich means both a crying child and a droplet of tears. The verse exploits the double meaning of these words to conjure up two different situations: one where the speaker laments his separation from wine and says that constant crying is now his lot and the other where he mourns separation from a woman who has left behind a crying child.

bastah shud har chand dar yak bahr ma'na haaye tar
ma'naye mardum habaab u ma'naye man gauhar ast

Though the sea harbours
meanings in plenty,
Mine is a pearl,
theirs a bubble.

The Persian for sea is *bahr*, which also means the metre in which verse is written. The verse simultaneously brings both meanings into play.

na daar-e aakhirat nay daar-e dunya dar nazar daaram
zi ishqat kaar chun Mansur ba daar-e digar daaram

Neither this abode I desire
nor the next one.
Like Mansur, in your love,
I desire one beyond both.

Again, the Persian *daar* means both abode and gibbet. In the context of the verse both are simultaneously implied, as Mansur by preferring to die on a gibbet also chose an abode beyond this world and the paradise of the orthodox.

heechgah lab nakunad baaz ba dushnaam-e raqeeb
man ba tang aamadam az yaar ki pur beedahan ast

Not once did she open her
mouth to curse the rival.
I am fed up of a love
so tight-lipped.

Translated here as tight-lipped, *bee-dahan* literally means 'mouthless'. In Persian poetry the smallness of the beloved's mouth is a mark of her beauty which, in keeping with the conventions of hyperbole, is sometimes compared to just a tiny dot. The verse draws on both meanings of *bee-dahan*, thus saying: Would that she were not so beautiful to attract the rival; and, would that she had the will to curse him! By this device the poet makes use of a verbal nuance which, in the words of William Empson, 'gives room for alternative reactions to the same piece of language'.[21] Unfortunately, the beauty of punning and wordplay is one among those things that are lost in translation.

Yet another outstanding feature of Ghani is his brilliant use of paradox. As the noted American critic Cleanth Brooks has observed, it is generally, and wrongly, assumed that paradox has no place in poetry. On the contrary, he argues, much of good poetry is fundamentally paradoxical. Brooks and some other New Critics regarded paradox central to poetry because of its ability to embody a truth about reality which scientific or rational discourse is unable to capture. Reality, in other words, is not amenable to a purely logical analysis, and poetry, by dealing with its contradictory and paradoxical aspects, performs a very important function. Ghani's poetry offers fascinating instances of the use of paradox:

So enfeebled that life
struggles to reach my lips,
The strength of my infirmity
keeps me alive.

Attempting to conceal,
I revealed the secret of my love.
The teeth of the stitch tore
asunder my veil.

How much more will water
thirst for a kiss at your feet?
O sapling of the garden of beauty,
raise it from the dust.

Prohibitor! Want to make
the wine maker redundant?
Better that you crush the
grape cups.

Deep prayer checks
the wandering mind.
Many locks are unlocked
by locked hands.

The above discussion would perhaps make it sufficiently clear that the strength of Ghani's poetry lies in working on familiar images to create novel and striking metaphors and poetic themes. If the classical Persian ghazal is centred on more or less a definite set of themes and images, which have kept recurring through the ages, then a poet's success lies primarily in creating something new from something very familiar.

In fact, one might say that the world of the ghazal is a world of certain typical situations and characters, which makes it a distinct genre of poetry. It is worthwhile to quote Faruqi and Pritchett in this regard:

> The human inhabitants of the ghazal universe are stylized, and exist chiefly to fulfill certain necessary functions: the lover's friends, his confidant, his rivals, his messenger, the beloved's cruel doorkeeper, the Shaikh full of reproachful and ostentatious piety, the Advisor with his unheeded words of caution, etc. The geography of the ghazal universe includes settings for the lover's every mood: the garden for dialogue between nature and man, the social gathering for human relationships, the wine-house for intoxication and mystic revelation, the mosque for ostentatious impiety, the desert for solitary wandering, the madhouse or prison cell for intransigence and frenzy, the grave and its aftermath for ultimate triumph or defeat. The ghazal universe is thus filled with beings and objects so 'pre-poeticized' that they bear only the most incidental relationship to their natural counterparts.[22]

The word ghazal itself means 'amorous talk', so it is not surprising that love is its primary theme. The speaker often expresses emotions of an unfulfilled longing and intense mental anguish, mostly due to the beloved's apathy and cruelty. The recurring images of the burning candle, doleful song, weeping eye, branded heart and torn garment reflect the conditions of thwarted desire and frustration. The beloved in the ghazal can be earthly or divine, both or neither, that is, the poet may simply be making use of the tradition rather than expressing any personal emotion. One needs to guard against the temptation to read the ghazal as a form of confessional autobiography and also resist the tendency to always identify the speaker with the poet. It is, therefore, quite probable that in celebrating drinking, eulogizing drinkers, castigating the prohibitor and the ascetic, and slighting religious rituals, Ghani is neither expressing his personal likes and dislikes nor obliquely alluding to the futility of religious observances, but merely making use of the conventional tropes of the ghazal to create poetry.

This caveat notwithstanding, it is nonetheless fruitful to look at Ghani's poetry in the light of whatever little can be established about his personality. As discussed earlier, Ghani's extreme austerity and other-worldliness have been reported by most literary historians as the defining features of his personality. It may not therefore be unjustified to argue that while his treatment of love and wine was probably determined by the long-established conventions of ghazal writing, his obsession with themes such as poverty and seclusion seems to have had its roots in his disposition and personal experiences.

Again, although Ghani's treatment of Sufi themes falls well within the conventions of the Persian ghazal, there is an unmistakable personal ring to many verses which allude to Sufi ideas of self-discipline, *fana*, or self-annihilation, the illusory nature of the world and the like. Mansur Hallaj (d. 922), the famous Sufi martyr celebrated by numerous Persian poets, is mentioned quite a few times:

As soon as Mansur spun his
thread from the cotton of Oneness,
The rosary and the infidel's thread
became one.

Neither this abode I desire
nor the next one.
Like Mansur, in your love,
I desire one beyond both.

Mansur bore himself away
and left the gibbet behind.
Mark, the rose is fled but
the thorn abides its place.

Ghani admiringly refers to the famous Sufi practice of *nafas shumardan*, or arresting one's breath:

> To rein in their selves
> is the jihad of men.
> To keep a count of their
> breaths the gnostics' task.

And one can find verses with deep mystical meaning scattered here and there in his *divan*:

> Alive none can know, Ghani,
> even in a dream,
> The solace that awaits
> the heart in the grave.

> In old age, Ghani, turn the
> dust to clay with tears
> And make your bent frame
> the mould for your grave's bricks.

> For those who embrace
> self-extinction, Ghani,
> Await beneath the earth joys
> unknown to those above it.

Despite these frequent allusions to mystical ideas it would seem rather inappropriate to attach the appellation 'Sufi poet' to Ghani or to call him simply a Sufi poet for various reasons. Firstly, unlike most Sufi poets, who tend to resort to the description of the physical world primarily to drive home some spiritual lesson, Ghani does not always seek a parallel between the physical and spiritual realms. Neither is he irresistibly drawn to celebrate the inner state. Instead, an overview of his whole poetic oeuvre reveals a consciousness caught in an unresolved conflict which often takes the form of pessimistic expression. This conflict is noticeable in the poet's simultaneous celebration of his humble state and frequent complaints against his fate and fellowmen, who are accused of apathy and indifference.

It is worthwhile to look for the causes that can help explain the presence of such a strong pessimistic strain in Ghani. It is reasonable to assume that the political and social unrest of Kashmir that he was witness to was primarily responsible for it. The political instability and subjugation by foreign powers must have had a severely negative impact on the collective consciousness of the Kashmiris. Already, before the Mughal conquest in 1586, Kashmir was torn by bloody internal strife between powerful chieftains and different religious sects. With the Mughal annexation, Kashmir lost its sovereignty and became yet another Mughal territory exploited fully to fill the treasuries at Agra and Delhi. The Mughals appointed numerous governors to the newly won state, most of whom were ruthless with the natives and adopted oppressive measures to extract different kinds of taxes from them. There exist several accounts, both in historical documents and literary texts, describing the dismal condition of the people due to these oppressive policies. Nadim Kashmiri, a contemporary of Ghani, presented in a *qasida*, or panegyric, written for the emperor Shah Jahan, an account of the humiliation Kashmiris faced at the hands of Itiqad Khan, the governor of Kashmir. To add further to their miseries, natural calamities in the form of floods and famines had become routine. It was only natural for Ghani to be deeply perturbed by these conditions and he imbibed the general mood of gloom and dejection. A psyche impinged by such awfully dismal spectacles was likely to seek vent in expressions of fatalism and pessimism. If Ghani seems too gloomy at times, it is because the conditions he lived in offered little reason for a brighter outlook. Perhaps these external factors actually intensified a pre-existing melancholic streak in him. And perhaps by saying that severity is best answered with soft-heartedness, he advises his people to tackle harshness with prudence:

> With tenderness you can escape
> the oppressors' clutches.
> Has the painter's brush ever
> come under the sword's edge?

> With softness we can save ourselves
> from the tyrants' grasp.
> Unlike pearls, water droplets fear not
> being strung into thread.

The following verses might as well be read as a telling indictment of the way people were fleeced:

> No falcon have I seen
> building a nest.
> Picking on birds serves as a
> substitute to gathering straw.

> Our sustenance is fated to fall
> to the others' lot.
> Like the millstone, our fortune
> often takes reverse turns.

> Like the needle we always
> flee from being dressed.
> Naked ourselves, we stitch
> garments for others.

It was this general plight of the Kashmiris that Iqbal was to bemoan in *Payaam-e Mashriq*:

Alas! So much has he
inured himself to servility
That from tombstones
the Kashmiri carves out idols.

No lofty thought finds
place in his mind.
Oblivious to his own lot,
of himself ashamed.

Clad in silk is his master
from his toil.
He himself is draped in
a tattered shirt.

His eyes are bereft of
the vision that discerns.
His breast is bereft of
a restless heart.

Disconcerting though it may seem to the modern reader, the
strain of dejection nonetheless affords poignancy to Ghani's verses:

Such desolation pours down from
the walls and doors, it seems
That the heavens have sketched
my house from the pallor of my face.

Beneath the earth lies the
abode of this dust-ridden one,
While the surface is full of
men seated aloft.

Ghani, I fear my misfortune
will afflict my trade,

If ever I take up the scales
for a petty profit.

For how long would Ghani have
his breast riddled with poverty?
With the thread of his robe
he stitched his torn breast.

From the cold indifference of the sky
I flee to ill luck.
May no one seek shade
in the wintry chill!

Nothing but remorse
does the world yield.
Turning the millstone
only chafes our hands.

Since poverty has come to inhabit my dwelling
The dust of hope has fled from this desolate abode.
It is not becoming to knock on others' doors today
When hunger has arrived as a guest at mine.

Despite a substantial number of such verses in Ghani, it would
be fallacious to describe him as a poet only of despair and gloom.
Ghani celebrates all positive facets of life with an unmistakable
note of imaginative delight. He has a penchant for concrete images
through which he proclaims his keen appreciation of the sensuous
forms of beauty. If our poet often bemoans his destitution or draws
from the fast-fading rose a lesson of life's transience, he also rejoices
in describing spring, tracing the sweetness of honey to a sweet lip
the bee has stung, vividly describing the biting cold of Kashmir's
winter and writing satirical verses on a barber.

It seems pertinent to conclude this introduction with a passage from Iqbal's celebrated work *Javed Nama* (1928), where the spirit of Ghani appears as a harbinger of deliverance from darkness and despair. In the course of his heavenly journey, Zinda Rud, who represents Iqbal, finds Ghani lamenting the state of his nation in these words:

> O morning breeze, if you
> pass over Geneva,
> Carry a word from us
> to the League of Nations.
>
> 'The peasant, the field, the river,
> the garden, all have they sold.
> They have sold a people and how
> cheaply have they sold!'

The reference is to the infamous Treaty of Amritsar signed in 1846, when the state of Jammu and Kashmir was sold along with its people by the British to the Dogra rulers. But soon Ghani's spirit predicts a future when Kashmir will regain the glory and pride of the past. Ghani inspires Zinda Rud with words that reveal his unflinching faith in his people's determination to live with honour and dignity:

> Do you think our soil
> is bereft of spark?
> Look into your heart
> with a keener eye.
>
> Wherefrom has passion
> and fervour come?
> Wherefrom has this breath
> of the spring's breeze come?

Introduction

It has come from the
very wind which
Bestows colour and scent
on our lofty mountains.

After a few lines he continues:

Your cry is a bell
waking up the caravans.
Why do you despair of
the people of this place?

Their breasts do not carry
dead hearts.
Their sparks are still
alive under the ice.

Wait till you see that
without the trumpet's blast
A whole nation will rise to
life from their graves.

Grieve not, O you gifted
with the vision.
Exhale the scorching breath
to consume the dry and the wet.

Under this turquoise sky
many a city has been torched
By the fire that exudes from
the dervish's heart.

A kingdom is flimsier
than a bubble.

It can be blown up
by a single breath.

It is the song that fashions
the destiny of nations.
A song can make or
mar nations.

Though men's hearts are
transfixed by your lancet,
None has discerned your
true worth yet.

Notes that emanate from you
are a poet's song,
But what you say goes
well beyond poetry.

Raise a fresh tumult
in Paradise.
Sing a song of drunkenness
in Paradise.

Mufti Mudasir Farooqi

Ghazals

1

junūnī kū ki az qaid-e khirad bīrūn kasham pā rā
kunam zanjīr-e pāye khwīshtan dāmān-e śaĥrā rā

ba bazm-e may parastān muĥtasib khush ʿizzatī dārad
ki chūn āyad ba majlis shīshah khālī mī kunad jā rā

agar shuhrat havas dārī asīr-e dām-e ʿuzlat shav
ki dar parvāz dārad gūshah gīrī nām-e ʿanqā rā

ba bazm-e may parastān sarkashī bar ṭāq nih zāhid
ki mīrīzand mastān bī muĥābā khūn-e mīna rā

shikast az har dar-u-dīvār mībārad magar gardūn
zi rang-e chahraye mā rīkht rang-e khānaye mā rā

Ghazals

1

O for a frenzy that could free
me from the bonds of reason
And chain my feet to the
edge of the desert!

In the company of wine lovers
the prohibitor enjoys high esteem,
For on his arrival goblets
are instantly emptied.[1]

If you desire fame, become
a prisoner of solitude's snare,
For seclusion is called phoenix
when it soars high.[2]

Ascetic, shelve your arrogance
in the drinkers' assembly.
Look! Drunk, how recklessly they
spill the flask's blood.[3]

Such desolation pours down from
the walls and doors, it seems
That the heavens have sketched
my house from the pallor of my face.

nadārad rah ba gardūn rūh tā bāshad nafas dar tan
rasāyī nīst dar parvāz murgh-e rishtah dar pā rā

Ghanī rūz-e siyāh-e pīr-e Kan'ān rā tamāsha kun
ki nūr-e dīdah ash raushan kard chashm-e Zuleikhā rā

2

mayār ay bakht bahr-e gharq-e mā dar shūr daryā rā
par-e māhī magar dān bādbān-e kashtiye mā rā

libās-e mā sabuksārān ta'alluq bar namī tābad
buvad hamchūn ḥabāb az bakhyah khāli pairahan mā rā

buvad az shu'la-e āwāz-e qulqul bazm-e may raushan
sarat gardam makun khāmūsh sāqi sham'-e mīnā rā

Trapped in the body
the soul cannot ascend.
With feet tied what bird
could take flight?

Ghani, behold the darkened days
of the old man of Canaan
As the light of his eyes now
illumines those of Zuleikha.[4]

2

To drown me, O Fate,
raise no storm in the sea.
Remember, my boat's sail
is but the fin of a fish.

Too flimsy to bear ties are
the apparels of the burdenless.
Like an air bubble my robes
are without a stitch.

The flame of gurgling wine irradiates
the wine gathering.
My life is yours, Saki,
let not the sparkling flask fall silent![5]

dam-e jān bakhsh-e ū tā rang-e ĥairat rīkht dar ʿālam
zi mihr-e āyinah dar pīsh-e nafas dīdam masīĥā rā

agar lab az sukhan gūyī farūbandīm jā dārad
ki nabvad az nazākat tāb-e bastan-e maʿnaye mā rā

Ghanī sāghar bakaf Jamshīd pīsh-e mayfarūsh āmad
ki shāyad dar bahāye bādah gīrad mulk-e dunyā rā

3

tihī kun ay dil az parvardaye khud zūd pahlū rā
ki ākhir nāfah tā kushtan buvad hamrāh-e āhū rā

nagardad shiʿr-e man mashhūr tā jān dar tanam bāshad
ki baʿd az marg-e āhū nāfah bīrūn mīdihad bū rā

No sooner had his life-infusing breath
held the world spellbound
Than I saw the messianic breath
brought to the mirror's test.[6]

How apt if I seal my lips
from saying verse!
For the subtlety of my meanings
lies well beyond them.

Cup in hand, Ghani, Jamshed
came to the wine seller.
Perchance in lieu of wine,
he asks for the whole world.[7]

3

Shun fast what you have
nurtured, O heart!
The musk-bag clings to
the deer until it is slain.[8]

Fame eluded my verse till the soul
was the body's prisoner.
The fragrant musk found release
once the deer was slain.

zi āsīb-e śabā āsūdah tā śubĥ-e abad bāshad
kunad shamʿ az par-e parvānah gar taʿvīż-e bāzū rā

ba narmī jān zi dast-e sakht gīrān mītavān burdan
bazīr-e tīgh hargiz kas nagīrad khāmaye mū rā

kunad dar pīsh-e ān pāye nigārīn sajdahā zulfash
balī karī bih az ātash parastī nīst Hindū rā

falak dar gardish ast az bahr-e khwāb-e bakht-e nāsāzam
buvad dar jumbish-e gahwārah rāĥat ṭifl-e badkhū rā

Ghanī az sustiye ṭāliʿ shikast uftad babāzāram
paye saudā bakaf gīram agar sang-e tarāzū rā

Safe from the curse of breeze
will it be till the morn of eternity,
If from the moth's wing
the candle fashions an amulet.[9]

With tenderness you can escape
the oppressors' clutches.
Has the painter's brush ever
come under the sword's edge?[10]

Her decked vermilion feet,
his endless prostrations.
What act, for a Hindu,
can excel the worship of fire!

The skies are in motion
to put my ill luck to sleep.
The rocking cradle brings
comfort to the fretful child.[11]

Ghani, I fear my misfortune
will afflict my trade,
If ever I take up the scales
for a petty profit.

4

tavānad śūratī dādan shabīh-e ān parī rū rā
musavvir gar kunad az bāl-e ʿanqā khāmaye mū rā

hizarān maʿanaye bārīk bāshad bayt-e abrū rā
ba ghair az mūshigāfān kas na fahmad maʿnaye ū rā

mayān-e kushtgān sar az khajālat bar namīdārīm
tihī tā chūn kamān kardīm az tīr-e tū pahlū rā

magar naqlī zi rūye nuskhaye ĥusn-e tū bardārad
ki mah imshab kashīd az hālah jadwal śafĥaye rū rā

Ghanī tā chand bāshad sīna chāk az dast-e ʿuryāni
ba tār-e pairahan dūzīd chāk-e sīnaye ū rā

4

The likeness of that fairy face
the painter can capture,
Only if he makes his brush
from the feathers of the phoenix.[12]

Thousands of meanings lie hidden
in the brow-shaped couplet.
Unfathomable to all
but the hair-splitters.

Shamed, I did not raise
my head amidst the slain.
Until, like the bow, I rid
my breast of your arrow.[13]

Perhaps it has copied the sketch
of your beautiful visage:
Tonight the moon's halo
seems drawn from a portrait.

For how long would Ghani have
his breast riddled with poverty?
With the thread of his robe
he stitched his torn breast.

5

zi rūye māh siyāhī ba nūr-e māh naraft
nayāmad ast ba kārī kamāl-e khwīsh marā

kasī ba pursish-e aḥvāl-e man namī āyad
ba ghair-e khandah ki āyad ba ḥāl-e khwīsh marā

zi ghunchah takyah chū shabnam ba zīr-e sar na niham
ki bih zi bālish-e par hast bāl-e khwīsh marā

basān-e shamʿ ki uftad zi pambaye khud ba gudāz
vabāl-e gardan-e khud gasht bāl-e khwīsh marā

ba gulshan-e digrī chashm-e man namī uftad
gul-e murād shiguft az sifāl-e khwīsh marā

5

The moon's lustre cannot
remove blackness from its face.
Alas, my talent stood me
in no good stead![14]

None comes to ask after me,
Except my own laugh
that comes to mock me.

Like a dewdrop I choose
no rosebud to recline.
Better than the feathered
pillow is my own wing.

Like the candle consumed
by its own wick,
My neck was undone
by its own wing.

I gaze not in envy
at the other's garden.
My desire's rose
blooms in my own clay.

6

chashm-e mā raushan shud az khāk-e dar-e maikhānahā
rīkhtand az surmah gūya rang-e īn kāshānahā

saʿī bahr-e rāĥat-e hamsāygān kardan khush ast
bishinvad gūsh az barāye khwāb-e chashm afsānahā

barham az sargarmiye mā khurd bazm-e maykashān
ātashī gashtīm u uftādīm dar maykhānahā

dar shab-e zulf-e tū khwāb-e khush naśībam kay shavad
khār mīrūyad zi pahlūyam ba sān-e shānahā

ātash-e dāgh-e junūn az sang-e ṭiflān mīkashand
yak nafas ghāfil nayand az kār-e khud dīvānahā

6

My eyes owe their vision
to the dust of tavern doors.
As if these abodes were raised
on antimony.[15]

Noble indeed it is to strive
for the neighbour's comfort.
The ear endures a hundred tales
that the eye may sleep.

Amidst the drinkers
our revelry raised a tumult.
Metamorphosed into flames,
we consumed countless taverns.

Entangled in your black tresses,
I pine for a restful sleep.
Like the teeth of the comb,
thorns issue from my breast.

To burnish the scar of their madness,
they draw the spark from urchins' stones.
Not for a moment are the frenzied
forgetful of their duty.[16]

raft 'umram dar gharībi bar bisāt-e rūzgār
garchi hamchūn muhraye shatranj dāram khānahā

ba'd-e murdan gar khūrad afsūs ān sarkash chi sūd
mī gazad angusht sham' az mātam-e parvānahā

dāyim az mastī Ghanī dar raqś chūn dūlāb bāsh
gar nabāshad may tavān kard āb dar paimānahā

7

mā bulbulān-e buland nasāzīm khānah rā
khush kardah-īm khānaye yak āshiyānāh rā

sangīn dil ast har ki ba źāhir mulāyam ast
pinhān darūn-e panbah nigar panbah dānah rā

An eternal exile
on the plane of existence,
Though like a draught
I have many homes.

What does it avail if
the heedless one repents after my death?
Does not the candle bite its finger
in grief for the moth?[17]

Like a waterwheel keep dancing
in rapture, Ghani.
If wine be scarce,
fill the goblets with water.

7

We, the nightingales of loftiness,
despise building nests.
One abode alone
affords us joy.[18]

Stone-hearted is he
who appears soft from without.
Behold the cotton seed
nestled inside the fluff.

shud sang-e āstānaye dīn har butī ki būd
kāfir biyā u sajdah kun īn āstānah rā

rūzī ki gul zi bāgh baghārat barad khizān
bulbul ba bād dih sabad-e āshiyānāh rā

andīshah gar zi tangiye gūrat buvad Ghanī
dar zindagī zi khāk bar āvar khazānah rā

8

shud khatm bar hadīṣ-e tū ākhir bayān-e mā
bāshad nigīn-e nām-e tū muhr-e dahān-e mā

tar hamchū āsiyā nashud az āb nān-e mā
az tishnagī ast khushk zabān dar dahān-e mā

Transmuted into a shrine's threshold
is every idol of the past.
Infidel, come and bow before it.[19]

The day autumn plunders
the rose from the garden,
Nightingale, give up
your nest to the storm.

If the narrowness of your grave
you fear, Ghani,
To give away the treasures
bring them out when alive.[20]

8

Your description puts
an end to all narration.
Your precious name becomes
the seal of my lips.

My loaf of bread stays
dry like the watermill,
Parched like my tongue
inside my mouth.

āgah nashud ṭabīb zi dard-e nihān-e mā
īn nabẑ-e mā khamūsh tar ast az zabān-e mā

gūyī ki dar tannūr-e falak qahṭ-e haizum ast
tā ishtihā nasūkht nashud pukhta nān-e mā

az baski vasf-e chashm-e siyāh-e tu kardah īm
gardīd mīl-e surmah zabān dar dahān-e mā

az śaidgah-e dahar nagashtīm nā umīd
zāgẖ-e kamān-e māst shikār-e kamān-e mā

mūye safīd-e māst hamah gard-e āsiyā
shud qūt-e āsiyāye falak ustukhān-e mā

The physician failed to catch
the ailment within.
The tongue was silent,
the pulse even more so.

The furnace of the sky was
short of firewood.
To bake my bread it
stokes itself with my desire.[21]

Engrossed such in praising
your dark eyes,
The tongue in my mouth has
turned a kohl stick.

The world's hunting ground
still holds a promise for me.
Searching for a prey,
my bow might hunt itself.

Scattered around the millstone
are my white strands.
Grains to the sky's revolving mill
are my bones.

kas rā zi dām-e śuĥbat-e mardum najāt nīst
'anqā ast gūshah gīr Ghanī dar zamān-e mā

9

bī nishāni dārad āzād az balā vārastah rā
dām bāshad naqsh-e pāye khwīsh śaid-e jastah rā

dar mukarrar bastan-e maẑmūn-e rangīn luṭf nīst
kam dihad rang ar kasī bandad ĥināye bastah rā

daf' shud vasvās-e khāṭir az namāz-e bā huẑūr
mā badast-e bastah vā kardīm qufl-e bastah rā

bī tū har shab tā saĥar dārad Ghanī sūz u gudāz
sham'-e bālīn shāhid-e ĥālast īn dil khastah rā

22

The snare of men's company
spares none.
Rare as a phoenix, Ghani,
is a recluse is now.

9

Leave no trail and
escape misfortune.
The footprints of a runaway
game become its trap.

An oft-repeated colourful
theme looks bland.
Faded indeed is the colour
of used henna.

Deep prayer checks
the wandering mind.
Many locks are unlocked
by locked hands.

From dusk to dawn every night,
Ghani burns for you.
Witness to my heartache
is the candle by my pillow.

10

safer chigūnah kunī az dayār-e khāṭir hā
ki dāman-e tū bigīrad ghubār-e khāṭir hā

zi bazm-e may buru ay muĥtasib ki dastārat
chu panbaye sar-e mīnāst bār-e khāṭir hā

chū mīl-e surmah bar āmad zi chashm-e jānān guft
ki sair-e maykadah shūyad ghubār-e khāṭir hā

11

jān rā ba kūye dūst ravān mīkunīm mā
ya'nī ki kār-e 'ishq ba jān mīkunīm mā

muṭrib gar ārzūye tū faryād-e mā buvad
mānand-e nay ba dīdah fighān mīkunīm mā

10

How can you come out of
the mesh of thoughts?
Clutching at your hem
are they in profusion.

Leave the wine assembly,
prohibitor, for your turban
Weighs upon my thoughts
like the stopper of the decanter.[22]

Coming out of the beloved's eye
the kohl stick remarked:
'A stroll through the tavern
wipes away the dust of thoughts.'

11

Life itself we send forth
into love's street,
And thus we perform
the duty of love.

Minstrel, if we too were to sing
of the heart's desire,
Like the flute we too would
give vent through the eye.

mashhūr dar savād-e jahān az sukhan shudīm
hamchūn qalam safar ba zabān mīkunīm mā

natavān chū zāhid az rāh-e khushkī ba Ka'ba raft
kashtī ba bahr-e bādah ravān mīkunīm mā

mārā chū sham' marg buvad khāmushī Ghanī
iẓhār-e zindagī ba zabān mīkunīm mā

12

yak sahar az daram ay davlat-e bīdār biyā
rūzam ay māh shudah bītū shab-e tār biyā

halqaye dar bingar rakhnaye dīwār bibīn
chashm dar rāh-e tū dārad dar-u-dīwār biyā

Round the world my verse
spreads my fame.
Like a pen, I journeyed
astride my tongue.

To Kaaba, the arid path
of the ascetic we shun.
And set sail our boat in
the sea of wine.[23]

Silence, as for the candle,
is death for us, Ghani.
Only by the tongue can
we display our existence.

12

O wakeful bounty, one morn
to my door, do come!
O moon, whose absence
darkens my days, do come!

Behold the knocker on the
door and the crevice in the wall.
The door and the wall of my
eyes await you, do come.[24]

'użr dar rāh-e vafā pīsh nakhwāhad raftan
bar sar-e 'użr mayā bar sar-e raftār biyā

13

i'timadī nīst bar gardūn ki dar vaqt-e binā
rīkht mi'mār-e qażā rang az shafaq īn khānah rā

tab'-e ān shā'ir ki shud bā ṭarz-e duzdī āshnā
ma'naye bīgānah dānad ma'naye bīgānah rā

chashm-e 'āshiq raushan ast az partav-e dīdār-e dūst
sham'-e nakhl-e vādi-e aiman buvad parvānah rā

'āshiqān rā mīshavad bakht-e siyāh żil-e humā
shu'la bar sar afsar-e shāhi buvad parvānah rā

Excuses shall not traverse
the path of love.
Shun them, make haste,
and do come.

13

Unpredictable are the firmaments
for at their creation's time,
The Designer of Fate drew
their sketch from the horizons.[25]

The poet whose nature
inclines to stealing
Remains obtuse to the novel
meaning he steals.

The eyes of the lover are illumined
by the beloved's reflection.
The candle becomes a tree
of refuge for the moth.[26]

For lovers, black fortune
becomes the huma's shadow.
For the moth, the flame
a kingly crown.[27]

14

har ki pāband-e vatan shud mīkashad āzār hā
pāye gul andar chaman dāyim pur ast az khār hā

hīchgah az sīnaye śad chāk-e mā yādī nakard
garchi bastam rishtah bar angusht-e sūzan bārhā

tā ba rūye gul nayaftad chashm-e bīrūn māndgān
bast bulbul āshiyān dar rakhnaye dīwār hā

zān lab-e mīgūn Ghanī rā bādaye dih sar bamuhar
kaz sarash bīrūn ravad bād-e hamah pindār hā

15

tāk shud zanjīr-e pāyam tā kashīdam bādah rā
'āqibat az dast dādam dāman-e sajjādah rā

14

Whoever holds firmly to
his soil bears affliction.
The feet of the rose are
ever fraught with thorns.

Not once did it think
of my myriad-holed breast,
Though I too have threaded
the needle many times.

Lest strangers cast their
devouring gaze on the rose,
In the wall's crevice has the
nightingale built its nest.

From those ruby lips pass,
Ghani, a sealed draught.
For he has thrown all
discretion to the wind.

15

I consumed so much wine
that my feet's chains turned into vine.
At last from my hand I threw
away the prayer mat.

sāyah mīgūyad ba gūsh-e naqsh-e pā dar har qadam
hīchkas dastī nagīrad bar zamīn uftādah rā

har ki būd az may parastān shud murīd-e man Ghanī
tā bar āb afgandam az dāman-e tar sajjādah rā

16

hilāl nīst ki nākhun zadast bar dil-e charkh
nivishtah miśra'-e abrū-e ū ba āb-e ṭilā

khalal paẕīr shud az ẕabt-e giryah nūr-e nigāh
zi āstīn gilah dārad chirāg-e dīdaye mā

'ibādati ba jahān bih zi khāksāri nīst
bih az vuẕū-e 'azīzān buvad tayammum-e mā

The shadow whispers into
the footprint's ears:
'None holds the hand
of those fallen into dust.'

Ghani, every wine lover has
become my disciple since
In contrition I flung the
prayer mat into the sea of wine.

16

Not a crescent, but a fingernail
engraved in the sky's heart.
The hemistich of her eyebrow
written in golden ink.

Stifled tears blur the eye's vision.
The lamp of my eye complains
of my sleeve.[28]

The humility of dust-dwellers
excels all worship.
Dust cleanses us more than
the ablution does others.

ba bakht-e tīrah gurīzam zi sard mihriye charkh
mabād sāyah nishīn kas ba mausim-e sarmā

17

ba bahr-e pur khaṭr-e ʿishq chūn kushāyim chashm
ki chūn ḥabāb nigāhi kunad kharāb marā

chu man ba baḥr-e tajarrud kas āshnā nabvad
yakī ast pairahan-u-pūst chūn ḥabāb marā

18

ṣafāi-e ḥusn-e butān mī tarāvad az dil
ba āb-e āyinah gūyī sirishtah shud gil-e mā

chunān ba yād-e sar-e zulf-e ū giriftārīm
ki ghair-e khānaye zanjīr nīst manzil-e mā

From the cold indifference of the sky
I flee to ill luck.
May no one seek shade
in the wintry chill!

17

Opening the eye in
love's tempestuous sea
Brought me to naught
like a bubble.

No one fathoms the sea of
nakedness like me.
Like the bubble my skin
and garment are one.

18

The idol's limpid beauty
permeates my heart.
As if my clay were
kneaded with crystal water.

Captivated by the memory
of her tresses,
I have no destination save
the rings of those chains.

shudīm khāk zi bas dar khayāl-e ʿāriẑ-e ū
sazad gar gul-e khurshīd rūyad az gil-e mā

19

mā rā az āftāb-e qayāmat Ghanī chi bāk
dūzakh tar ast az ʿarq-e infiʿāl-e mā

20

jahān tamām musakhkhar zi jām shud Jam rā
bigīr jām ki khwāhī girift ʿālam rā

Ghanī chirā śilaye shiʿr az kasī gīrad
hamīn bas ast ki shiʿrash girift ʿālam rā

The thought of her cheek
has turned me to clay.
Befitting that a sunflower
grows out of my soil.

19

What fear of the Resurrection Day's
sun can I have,
When hell is drenched by
the sweat of my humility?[29]

20

The whole world lies
in Jamshed's cup.
Seize the cup if you
desire the world.

Why should Ghani seek the
reward of verse from anyone?
It is enough that the world
seeks his verses.

21

chirā kham gashtah mī gardand pīrān-e jahān dīdah
magar dar khāk mī jūyand ayyām-e javānī rā

22

ma'nī az tab'-e Ghanī sar natavānad pīchīd
bastah dādand ba ū rūz-e azal maẑmūn rā

23

ba manzil mīrasanad kashtiye may kārvānī rā
barad yakdam azīn 'ālam ba ān 'ālam jahānī rā

24

sukhan muhr-e khamūshi bar namī dārad zabānash rā
ki lab chūn ghunchah pinhānast az tangī dahānash rā

21

Pray, why are the backs
of old men bent?
Are they searching for their
lost youth in the dust?

22

Meaning cannot refuse
submission to Ghani's genius.
Poetic themes were fashioned
for him at the dawn of creation.

23

The boat of wine steers the
caravan to its destination,
Ferrying one from this world
to that in no time.

24

Speech cannot break the seal
of silence from her tongue.
Like a rosebud her lip lies
hidden in her mouth.

25

khusham ki ẑuʿf chunān kard rūshinās marā
ki chashm-e āyinah miĵgān kunad qayās marā

26

zi dard-e ʿishq ẑaʿīf ast baski paikar-e mā
shavad ba tīgh-e girībān judā zi tan sar-e mā

27

tishnaye pā būs-e khud zīn bīsh magẕār āb rā
ay nihāl-e bāgh-e ĥusn az khāk bardār āb rā

28

biyā bulbul bibīn dar pardaye gul āftābī rā
chirā az sādgī maĥbūb-e khud kardī naqābī rā

25

Happy that weakness
made me so conspicuous
That the mirror's eye
took me for an eyelash!

26

The pangs of love have
so enfeebled my frame
That the garment's edge
can sever my head.

27

How much more will water
thirst for a kiss at your feet?
O sapling of the garden of beauty,
raise it from the dust.

28

Come, O nightingale, behold
a sun veiled in a rose.
Why, out of modesty,
do you hold your veil dear?

29

hamchūn sūzan dāyim az pūshish gurīzānīm mā
jāmah bahr-e khalq mī dūzīm u ʿuryānīm mā

30

tā bakht-e vāĵgūn shud miʿmār-e khānaye mā
gardīd chūn kamān kaj dīvār-e khānaye mā

31

ātash-e may tīz sāzad shuʿla-e āvāz rā
bar kadūye bādah bāyad bast tār-e sāz rā

32

khammār śāf az durd bahr-e tū kard may rā
āvard shauq-e laʿlat birūn zi pardah may rā

29

Like the needle we always
flee from being dressed.
Naked ourselves, we stitch
garments for others.

30

Since inverted fortune has
become the builder of my abode,
The walls of my house are
bent like a bow.

31

The spark of wine sharpens
the flame of sound.
Befitting that the lute be
tied to the wine gourd.

32

For you the vintner
cleared the wine of its dregs.
Desiring your ruby lips the
wine threw off its veil.

33

zūr-e may tā hast kay uftādah mī bāshīm mā
hamchūn khum dar gūr ham istādah mī bāshīm mā

34

tābūt-e murdaye dūsh hushyār kard mā rā
pāye ba khwāb raftah bīdār kard mā rā

35

khwīsh rā bā ki bisanjīm Ghanī dar sabukī
nīst juz sāyaye khud sang-e tarāzū mā rā

36

ḥusn-u-jamāl-e z̤āti ast dushman-e zīb-e ʿārẑi
surmah ghubār-e khāṭir ast chashm-e siyāh-e yār rā

33

How can we fall while
the effect of wine remains?
Like the wine jar we shall
stand erect even in the grave.[30]

34

The coffin of yesterday's dead
brought me to my senses.
The feet gone to sleep
woke me up.

35

To whom should I compare
myself in lightness, Ghani?
Apart from my shadow
I have no other measure.

36

Natural beauty is an
enemy of embellishment.
The kohl weighs heavy
upon her dark eyes.

37

sayyād-e mā chū tarkash pur tīr mī kunad
dar yak qafas asīr kunad śad parindah rā

38

sham'-e fānūs nayam līk zi bī sāmānī
ghair-e dīvār-e sarā pairahanī nīst marā

39

az rah-e vārastagi paivastah hamchūn girdbād
khānah bar dūsham namī bāshad gham-e manzil marā

40

pairav-e mā shav ki hamchūn khāmah dar rāh-e sukhan
pay ba ma'nī mītavān burdan zi naqsh-e pāye mā

37

Our hunter fills his
quiver with arrows,
And a hundred birds
he captures in a single cage.

38

Though not a candle in
the lantern yet, like it,
I own no garments but
the walls of my house.

39

Like the whirlwind, I am
ever free from bonds.
Abode on back, I have
no worries of settling down.

40

In the path of composition
be my disciple, for like the pen's trace,
My footprints may lead
you to the heart of meaning.

41

śāhib-e sukhan najumbad az bahr-e qūt az jā
dāyim ba khānaye khud rūzī rasad zabān rā

42

shab-e firāq-e tū ay āftāb-e 'ālamtāb
labāb ast chū gardūn zi dāgh sīnaye mā

43

tā dam az hamsariye zulf-e tū zad
mīgazad mār zabān-e khud rā

44

parvanah gū bimīr zi ghairat ki sham' rā
raushan kunand khalq ba khāk-e mazār-e mā

41

From his place the poet
moves not for sustenance.
In its cavern is the
tongue provided for!

42

The night of separation,
O world-illumining sun!
Like the firmament my breast
is teeming with scars!

43

That it could boast of
matching your tresses,
Into two the serpent
split its tongue.

44

Tell the moth to perish out
of shame, for the candle
Is lit by men from
the dust of our graves.

45

tā tavānī ʿāshiq-e maʿshūq-e harjāyī mashav
mīkunad khurshīd sargardān gul-e khurshīd rā

46

marg gavārā shavad mūy chū gardad safīd
lażżat-e digar buvad khwāb-e dam-e śubĥ rā

47

mulāyam mīshavad dar guftgū har kas ki kāmil shud
ki dāyim pambah bāshad dar dahān mināye pur may rā

48

jāmam ba ghair-e kāsaye zānūye fikr nīst
bāshad khāyal-e tāzah sharāb-e kuhan marā

45

Make not the fickle one
your beloved.
A wanderer does the sun
make of the sunflower.

46

When hair turns white
death becomes bearable.
The dream at dawn yields
a pleasure of its own.

47

An accomplished man
is soft-spoken.
Cotton plugs the mouth
of a filled flask.

48

I know of no goblet save my
frame cupped in reflection.
Every new thought becomes
old wine for me.[31]

49

ba chashm-e kam mabīn dar nāmaye a'māl-e mā zāhid
ki mībārad azīn abr-e siyāh bārān-e raĥmat hā

50

az sharm-e taubah dar 'araqam kū sharāb-e nāb
bāyad matā'-e tar shudah rā dād āftāb

raftīm sūye yār u nadīdīm rūye yār
mānand-e rahravī ki ravad rū ba āftāb.

tā kay farīb-e hastiye mauhūm mī khūrī
natavān chū 'aks-e āyīnah shud gharq dar sarāb

dar ĥashr shud bar ahl-e gunāh abr-e raĥmatī
andākhtam chū dāman-e tar rā ba āftāb

49

Slight not, O ascetic, my
blotted record of deeds.
Rains of mercy pour forth
from these black clouds.[32]

50

Soaked in shame over repentance;
pray, where is pure wine?
Things that are drenched
need the blazing sun.[33]

I marched towards my love
but could not see her face,
Like the wayfarer
who walks into the sun.

How long will you be deceived
by the world's illusion?
Like a mirror image, a mirage
can drown none.

The cloud of mercy shall cover
the sinners on Resurrection Day.
For I have thrown my drenched
garments into the sun.

khush davlatī ast faqr ki dar kunj-e inzivā
farsh-e nay ast sāyah u farrāsh āftāb.

har kas ki dād tan ba balā ayman az balā ast
vīran kujā zi mauj shavad khānaye ḥabāb

gar khāmah rā zi kām bar āyad zabān chi dūr
shud bahr-e shiʻr khushk tar az jadwal-e kitāb

tā bar nayāmad ast zi kāmam zabān Ghanī
charkh-e siyāh kāsah chū kilkam nadād āb

51

ādam-e khāki zi khāmī dārad az may ijtināb
kūzaye gil pukhtah chūn gardad namī tarsad zi āb

Pleasant is the wealth of poverty,
for in the corner of seclusion,
Shade is my reed mat and
my attendant, the sun.[34]

He who surrenders to calamity
has no fear from it.
How can the wave destroy
the bubble's house?

What wonder if my pen's
tongue drops out of its mouth?
The sea of verse has turned
drier than a book's sketch.

Until my tongue hangs out
from my mouth, Ghani,
Like my pen, the sky's
black bowl pours not a drop.

51

Abstinence is the trait
of unripe men.
The cup fully baked
has no fear of water.

har ki dar rāh-e sabuksāri qadam zad chūn ĥabāb
hīch jā pāyash na laghzad gar ravad bar rūye āb

dukhtar-e raz az nigāh-e garm uftād dar ĥijāb
kāsh uftādī gil-e abrī ba chashm-e āftāb.

az khajālat bar namī dārad chū nargis sar zi pīsh
har kirā faśl-e bahārān nīst dar sāghar sharāb

zāhid-e bī ābrū gar bar lab-e daryā ravad
mīshavad mauj-e ĥaśīr az zuhd-e khushkash mauj-e āb

sard mihrī baski dar dilhāye mardum jā girift
rūye garm az kas namī bīnam ghair az āftāb

He who is light-footed on
his path, like a bubble,
Walks sure-footed on
the water's surface.

From its fiery gaze the daughter
of vine hid behind the veil.
Would that a sore of a cloud
afflicts the sun's eye![35]

Like the narcissus his
head droops out of shame,
Whose cup is empty of wine
even in the spring.

If the ascetic, lacking self-esteem,
chances to go to the riverbank,
His arid asceticism will dry up
the wave like a mat.

Such cold indifference has
found place in men's hearts,
I see no warm face
except the blazing sun.

tā Ghanī kard ijtināb az mayparastān bīkhudī
gasht ʿaql-e mā ba rang-e nashah pinhān dar sharāb.

52

zi bīm-e hijr u umīd-e viṣāl-e ān maĥbūb
gudākht khāmah u bālīd dar kafam maktūb

khiẑāb-e mūye Zuleikhā magar kunad Yūsuf
ki burdah ast siyāhī zi dīdaye Yaʿqūb

havāye gūshah nishīnī agar paẑīrad rang
tavān basan-e kamān sākht khānaye yak chūb

Ghanī chū śiĥn-e chaman dar bahār rangīn ast
shabīh-e khāmaye naqqāsh mīshavad jārūb

Ghani, since drunkenness has
bid farewell to wine lovers,
My reason, like intoxication, has
hid itself in wine.

52

Afflicted by her separation,
the pen consumes away.
Expecting her union,
the letter blooms in my hand.[36]

No wonder that Yusuf
dyes Zuleikha's tresses:
He has stolen blackness
from Yaqub's eyes.[37]

If the desire for seclusion
takes a strong hold of you,
Like the bow an abode can
be carved from a single wood.

In spring, Ghani, the garden
blooms with myriad colours.
And the gardener's broom
resembles the painter's brush.

53

nafas-e man shudah az sūkhtgī khākistar
gar shavad āyīnah raushan zi dam-e man chi ʿajab

54

miĵa am bar miĵa az jūsh-e ĥalāvat chaspīd
dīdam az baski ba khwāb ān lab-e shīrīn imshab

55

dar namakzār-e savād-e Hind shādābī kam ast
gar darānja sabzaye bāshad zi tukhm-e ādam ast

gulshan-e Kashmīr rā imsāl shādābī kam ast
gar gil-e abrī numāyān ast ānham bī nam ast

53

Burning, my soul has
turned into ashes.
What wonder if my
breath polishes the mirror![38]

54

The ardour of sweetness
glued my lids together.
Tonight I dreamt of
that honeyed lip!

55

The brackish plains of India
are bereft of any freshness.
Verdure there, if any, grows
from the seeds of men.

The garden of Kashmir too
lacks verdure this year.
If a speck of cloud appears,
that too is bereft of moisture.

az badanhā dar havāye garm mī jūshad ʿaraq
gar buvad khāk-e raṭūbat khīz khāk-e ādam ast

dar jahān natavān nishān az sīr chashmī yāftan
chashmaye khurshīd ham muĥtāj-e āb-e shabnam ast

gard-e gham shūyad zi dilhā giryah dar bazm-e simāʿ
hast dar faryād chashm-e nay ki khāli az nam ast

56

mūye sar kardam safīd ammā khayālat dar sar ast
akhgarī pinhān tah-e īn tūdaye khākistar ast

az khadangat murgh-e dil pahlū ba tarkash mīzanad
kaz darūn yakdastah paikān vaz birūn musht-e par ast

Hot winds drain sweat
from men's bodies.
The only clay exuding
moisture is the clay of men.

It is hard to come across
a satiated eye in the world.
The sun's eye is ever thirsty
for a dewdrop.

In the musical gathering tears cleanse
the dust of grief from hearts.
Complaining of dryness, the flute's
eye raises laments.

56

White-haired, yet I
harbour thoughts of you.
In the heap of ashes
lives a spark.

Your arrows have turned
the heart into a quiver.
Arrowheads inside and
tufts of feathers hanging out.

kas zi faiẑ-e baĥr-e jūdash dar jahān maĥrūm nīst
pusht-e māhī pur diram musht-e śadaf pur gauhar ast

bastah shud har chand dar yak baĥr ma'na hāye tar
ma'naye mardum ĥabāb u ma'naye man gauhar ast

mī kunad khurshīd u mah āyīnah dārī sāyah rā
bā siyāh bakhtān butān rā iltifāt-e dīgar ast

57

pīr shud zāhid u az rāz-e darūn bī khabar ast
qad-e kham gashtaye ū ĥalqaye bīrūn-e dar ast

ĥairatam kusht ki chūn az sar-e 'ushāq guẓasht
āb-e shamshīr ki khūn rīz marā tā kamar ast

All partake of His sea of bounty.
With gold coins the fish is decked
and the oyster holds a pearl.

Though the sea harbours
meanings in plenty,
Mine is a pearl,
theirs a bubble.

The black-fortuned are
especially favoured by gods.
The sun and the moon are
ever attendant upon the shade.

57

Aged, yet the ascetic knows
not the inner secret.
His bent figure like the
knocker outside the door.

Wonder struck me dead
as the blood-spilling sword
Passed over the lovers' heads
to reach my waist.

zihr-e chashm-e tū chunān kard sarāyat dar man
ki marā pūst ba tan sabz chū bādam-e tar ast

nāvak-e nāz-e tū dar dīdaye man jā dārad
tīr-e mijgān-e turā mardum-e chashmam sipar ast

har ki pursīd zi Ghanī vajh-e shikast-e rangam
dānam az sang dilī hāye butān bī khabar ast

58

tā surmah dān siyāhiye chashm-e tū dīdah ast
dar chasm-e khwīsh mīl zi khijlat kashīdah ast

sūz-e dilam chū shamʿ ba jāye rasīdah ast
kaz tukhm-e ashk-e man gul-e ātash damīdah ast

Into my frame has your
poisonous glance sunk,
And turned my skin green
as a fresh almond.

My eye fears not the
darts of your charm.
Its pupil becomes the shield
for the arrows of your lashes.

He who asks you, Ghani,
the cause of your pallor
Knows not, I know,
how stone-hearted idols are.

58

Since the kohl vial has
glimpsed your black eyes,
In chagrin has it held back
the kohl stick.

Like the candle my heart's
passion has reached its end.
My streaming tears keep
the embers glowing.

gardīd rāz-e 'ishq zi pūshīdan āshkār
dandān-e bakhyah pardaye mā rā darīdah ast

qūs-e qazah agarchi ba gardūn kashīdah sar
abrūye yār dīdah u rangash parīdah ast

yak mūye farq nīst mayān-e dū abrū at
khush miśra'-e ba miśra'-e dīgar rasīdah ast

zin pīshtar ḫalāvat-e shahad īnqadar nabūd
zanbūr dānam ān lab-e shīrīn gazīdah ast

uftād gul zi dīdaye Ya'qūb hamchū ashk
dānam nasīm-e Miśr ba Kan'ān vazīdah ast

Attempting to conceal,
I revealed the secret of my love.
The teeth of the stitch tore
asunder my veil.

Brandishing itself against
the sky, the rainbow
Lost colour at the sight
of my love's eyebrows.

The exquisite similitude
of your eyebrows:
One hemistich as
elegant as the other.

Never before has honey
tasted so sweet.
The bee, I know, has
stung that sweet lip.

Like tears Yaqub sheds
affliction off his sore eyes.
The zephyr of Egypt has,
I know, set out for Canaan.[39]

dar ĥairatam ki āyinah imrūz śubĥ-e dam
rūye ki dīdah ast ki rūye tū dīdah ast

dar zindagī ba khwāb na bīnad kasī Ghanī
āsāyishī ki dil zi pas-e marg dīdah ast

59

sarnāmaye maktūb-e tū sar rishtaye kīn ast
saṭrīki darīn nāmah buvad chīn-e jabīn ast

āsūdah am az garmīye khurshīd-e qayāmat
kaz luṭf-e tū har nāmaye siyāh sāyāh nishīn ast

bar rūye zamīn hīchkas āsūdah nabāshad
ganjī buvad ārām ki dar zīr-e zamīn ast

What is it with the mirror
this morning?
Has it beheld a face?
Yours I'm sure.

Alive, none can know, Ghani,
even in a dream,
The solace that awaits
the heart in the grave.

59

The epigraph of your letter
tells of your pique.
Every line in it
a crease of the brow.

Of the doomsday's sun
I have no fear.
Your mercy makes a canopy
of my black deeds.[40]

The surface of the earth
provides no one comfort.
Peace is the real treasure
found beneath the earth.

mā zindagī az dīdan-e rukhsār-e tū dārīm
ākhir nigāh-e mā nafas-e bāz pasīn ast

kārī ba falak mardum-e āzādah nadārand
har sarv ki dīdam Ghanī khāk nishīn ast

60

bālish-e khūbān-e digar az par ast
shaukh-e marā fitnah ba zīr-e sar ast

pīsh-e lab-e yār ki jān parvar ast
har ki zanad dam zi Maśīha khar ast

bar lab-e khamyāzah kasham dar khumār
bakhyah agar hast khaṭ-e sāghar ast

Constantly gazing at you:
in this lives my life.
The last glance at you
is my last breath too.

Free men have no
business with the sky.
Every cypress we see, Ghani,
is grounded in the earth.[41]

60

Other beauties have their
pillows made of feathers.
My proud one harbours
mischief under hers.

When face-to-face with her
life-enhancing lips,
He who boasts of Christ's
breath is senseless.[42]

As ebriety departs, my
mouth is left agape.
Only the cup's brim
can stitch the void.

bī rukhat az baski nadārad śafā
āyinah gūyā kaf-e raushangar ast

āb buvad ma'naye raushan Ghanī
khūb agar bastah shavad gauhar ast

61

tā kār-e tū bīdāriye shabhāye darāz ast
chashmat dar-e faizī ast ki bar rūye tū bāz ast

uftādan u barkhāstan-e bādah parastān
dar mazhab-e rindān-e kharābāt namāz ast

may nīst chū dar kāsah marā ra'shah dar a'źā ast
dastam ba naźar panjaye ṭanbūr navāz ast

Deprived of your visage,
it has lost all sheen.
The mirror now looks
like the polisher's hand.

Luminous meaning is
water, Ghani.
Compactly knit, it turns
into a pearl.

61

Occupied with long vigils
during long nights,
Your eye is an ever-open
door of bounty on your face.

The rising and falling
of tipsy drinkers
Is namaz in the creed
of the tavern's dissolutes.[43]

No wine in the cup,
yet my limbs tremble,
My hands like those
of the lute player.

chūn bāl kushāyam ki darīn śaidgah-e dahar
az dām hamah rūye zamīn sīnaye bāz ast

62

chūn āstīn hamīshah jabīnam zi chīn pur ast
ya'nī dilam zi dast-e tū ay nāznīn pūr ast

har chashm-e nay zi naghmaye shīrīn labālab ast
zanbūr khanah īst ki az angbīn pur ast

har kas ba dargah-e karamat burd tuhfah ī
mā rā zi dast-e khāliye khud āstīn pur ast

juz zīr-e khāk jāye man-e khāksār nīst
rūye zamīn zi mardum-e bālā nishīn pur ast

As I stretch my wings over
the world's hunting ground,
To ensnare me, the earth's
breast is agape.

62

Like the sleeve my forehead
is always full of creases.
That is, O charming one,
my heart is etched with your palm.

Every eye of the flute
overflows with sweet melodies.
As each honeycomb of the
hive oozes honey.

All received gifts at
your bountiful shrine.
My sleeve too is full,
though only with my empty hand.

Beneath the earth lies the
abode of this dust-ridden one,
While the surface is full of
men seated aloft.

63

baski mānand-e paikaram az pīrī kāst
tā nagīrad kamram kas natavānam barkhāst

tā nasūzad nakunad mail-e bulandī chū sipand
chashm-e bad dūr azīn akhtar-e ṭāliʿ ki mar ast

gar kasī may nakharad gham makhūr ay bādah farūsh
īn matāʿ īst ki chūn kuhnah shavad bīsh bahā ast

ʿumr hā shud ki ba girdāb-e junūn uftādīm
kaf-e īn baĥr-e pur āshūb zi maghz-e sar-e mā ast

64

shiʿr agar iʿjāz bāshad bī buland u past nīst
dar yad-e baiẑā hamah angusht hā yak dast nīst

63

Decrepitude has turned
my frame into a bow.
I can't rise unless held by my waist.

Like wild rue, it rises
only when it burns.
May my auspicious star
be safe from the evil eye![44]

Grieve not, wine seller,
if none buys your wine.
It gets richer as it grows in age.

Ages have passed since I fell
into the whirlpool of madness.
My agitated mind raises foam
in this sea of tumult.

64

Exquisite verse too has
its ups and downs.
And the fingers of the
shining hand too vary in length.[45]

ay dil az mauj-e sarāb-e narmiye dushman bitars
bahr-e māhi halqa hāye dām kam az shast nīst

tā sarash az būye may shud garm khumhā rā shikast
hīchkas dar daur-e mā chūn muĥtasib badmast nīst

65

khāk az tīgh-e firāqam ba jigar zakhmī dāsht
kafanam marĥam-e kāfūr bar ān zakhm guzāsht

tuhmat-e khānah nishīnī na pasandīd ba khwīsh
varnah Majnūn gilah az sakhtiye zanjīr nadāsht

bar nadārīm zi ashʿār-e kasī maẑmūn rā
tabʿ-e nāzuk natāvanad sukhan-e kas bardāsht

O heart, beware of the mirage
of the enemy's gentleness.
No less than a sharp hook
is the fine net for the fish.

Inflamed by the wine's aroma
he shattered countless jars.
None in our gathering was more
deeply drunk than the prohibitor.

65

The sword of my separation
wounds the earth's heart.
And with camphor my shroud
dresses that wound.[46]

He could not bear being
called the 'settled one'.
Why else did Majnun
complain of the confining chain?[47]

From no one do I borrow
the theme of my poetry.
For a delicate disposition
others' speech is a burden.

tanash az tīr-e jafāye tū naistān gardīd
ʿalam-e shīr dilī har ki ba ʿālam afrāsht

66

maʿnaye śāf ki dar qālib-e alfāź-e bad ast
hast āyinah-e śāfi ki nihān dar namd ast

gar zi dam sardiye īn tīrah dilān āgah nīst
az chi rū jāmaye āyinah qabāye namd ast

tā shud angusht numā ṭurra at az ĥusn-e qabūl
shānah bar gīsuye khūbān-e digar dast rad ast

khāk rā gil bikun az giryah Ghanī dar pīrī
ĥalqaye qāmat-e kham qālib-e khisht-e laĥad ast

Like a reed bed, his body is
riddled with the arrows of your betrayal.
He who hoisted the flag
of bravery in the world.

66

Crystal meaning in the
mould of hazy words
Is like a mirror
wrapped in felt.

If the coldness of these indifferent
souls the mirror has not felt,
Pray why has it donned
the mantle of felt!

Since your forelock has become
the cynosure of admiration,
The comb has spurned
the tresses of other beauties.

In old age, Ghani, turn the
dust to clay with tears
And make your bent frame
the mould for your grave's bricks.

67

tār-e zulf-e yār az changash magar uftādah būd
shānah dar faryād imshab kam zi mūsīqār nīst

rishtah rā az panbaye tauĥīd tā Manśūr bāft
ikhtilāfī darmiyān-e subĥah u zunnār nīst

68

'inān-e nafs kashīdan jihād-e mardān ast
nafas shumardah zadan kār-e ahl-e 'irfān ast

marīz āb-e rukh-e khud barāye nān zinhār
ki ābrū chu shavad jam' āb-e ĥaivān ast

balā ast nafs 'inān chūn zi dast-e 'aql girift
'aśā chū az kaf -e Mūsa futad śu'bān ast

67

Perhaps the strings of the beloved's
tresses have grown from a lute,
For tonight the comb plays
like a musician.

As soon as Mansur spun his
thread from the cotton of Oneness,
The rosary and the infidel's thread
became one.[48]

68

To rein in their selves
is the jihad of men.
To keep a count of their
breaths the gnostics' task.[49]

Fritter away not the sweat
of your honour for mere bread.
The brow's sweat collects
and makes the elixir of life.

Deprived of reason's hold,
the self turns into a monster.
A serpent arose when the
staff fell from Musa's hand.[50]

mu'attar ast dimāgham zi khurdan-e śahbā
magar piyālah am imshab sifāl-e raihān ast

69

ba chashm-e khud natavān dīd śubĥ-e pīrī rā
khusham ki dīdah zi mū pīshtar safīd shud ast

70

darvīsh ba sāmān ki ravān shud nabarad jān
barg-e safar-e ahl-e qanā'at par-e mūr ast

bā murdah dilān chand nishīnī ba masājid
khum khānah nishīn bāsh ki khum zindah ba gūr ast

With fragrance has the wine
suffused my being tonight.
Sweet basil's earth, it seems,
was used to mould the cup.

69

One can't bear the sight of
the dawn of one's old age.
Happy that my eye turned
white before my hair!

70

Weighed down by other burdens,
no dervish can carry his soul.
An austere man's provision
is but an ant's wing.

How long will you sit in the
mosque amidst dead hearts?
Turn to the tavern, for the wine jar
lives even in the grave.

71

dāyim ba rāh-e shauq jilu rīz mīravad
gulgūn-e ashk rā mija am tāzyānah īst

ghāfil mashav zi 'āqibat-e kār-e khud Ghanī
dil nih ba khwāb-e marg ki dunyā fasānah īst

72

dil munawwar kay shavad dar żulmat ābād-e badan
sham' rā raushan namīsāzand tā dar qālib ast

zindah natavān būd bī la'lat ki mushtāq-e turā
yā lab-e shīrīn-e tū yā jān-e shīrīn bar lab ast

dānaye dām-e malāyik bar zamīn uftādah ast
kas namī dānad dur-e gūsh ast yā khāl-e lab ast

71

At a bridle-spurning speed,
they are always racing
in love's path.
For my rosy tears the
eyelashes are no less than whips.

Not for a moment be
unmindful of your end, Ghani.
Give yourself up to death's sleep,
for the world is an illusion.

72

Confined in the body's dark
chamber, the heart gains no light.
No candle glows until
taken out of its mould.

Parted from your lips, the lover's
life is slipping away.
If not your sweet lips,
his sweet life is on his lips.

The grain of beauty's snare
is lying on the ground.
Is it a pearl in the earlobe
or a mole on the lip?

73

takyah tā chand kunī bar nafasī hamchū ĥabāb
chashm bukshāyi ki hastī girahī bar bād ast

74

kulbaye mā garchi bī rauzan chū fānūs ast līk
bazm-e yārān az chirāgh-e khānaye mā raushan ast

shamʿ mīgūyad ba ahl-e bazm bā sūz-u-gudāz
sar burīdan pīsh-e īn sangīn dilān gulchīdan ast

nīst juz afsūs khurdan ĥāsil-e kisht-e jahān
āsiyā gardāniye mā dast barham sūdan ast

73

How long will you bank
on a mere breath like a bubble?
Open your eyes: life
is an airy knot.

74

Like the lantern,
my cottage is windowless.
Yet my lamp brightens
the gathering of friends.

Of these stone-hearted the candle
tearfully complains to the gathering:
'Severing heads for them
is akin to plucking flowers.'

Nothing but remorse
does the world yield.
Turning the millstone
only chafes our hands.

75

gūsh-e ghavvāś shunīd az lab-e khāmūsh-e ĥabāb
dam nigahdār kazīn bih guhrī natavān yāft

76

chunān ān nāznīn nāzuk dimāgh ast
ki ū rā būye gul dūd-e chirāgh ast

77

ʿāshiqān rā junbish-e mijɡān-e chashm-e yār kusht
ʿālamī rā iẑtirāb-e nabẑ-e īn bīmār kusht

tā shavad qabrash ziyārat gāh-e arbāb-riyā
khwīsh rā zāhid ba zīr-e gunbad-e dastār kusht

75

The silent lips of the bubble
whispered into the diver's ears:
'A pearl more precious
you shall never find.'

76

For her the fragrance of the
rose is the lamp's smoke.
So delicately made
is that graceful one.

77

The beloved's fluttering eyelashes
have slain many a lover.
This sick man's restive pulse
has slain the world.

Under his dome-like turban
the ascetic had himself killed,
That his tomb may become a
shrine for the pretentious.[51]

78

paivastah dilam śāf zi gard-e khaṭ-e yār ast
jārūb kash-e khānaye āyīnah ghubār ast

ma'żūr buvad zāhid agar jām na gīrad
kaz dānaye tasbīĥ kafash āblah dār ast

79

bī chirāgh ast agar bazm-e khayālam gham nīst
miśra'-e rīkhtah sham'ī st ki dar 'ālam nīst

gar muyassar nashud asbāb-e nishāṭam gham nīst
pīsh-e man chīn-e jabīn az lab-e khandān kam nīst

78

The dust of the beloved's down
keeps my heart ever clean.
The dust thus plays the
sweeper for my glasshouse.

The ascetic be excused if he
doesn't seize the cup.
Turning beads, his hand
is full of blisters!

79

Why grieve if my thought's
assembly is without a lamp?
Every well-wrought verse
is a matchless candle therein.

Why grieve if there's
none to cheer me up?
Her brow bedecked with
a frown is no less than a smiling lip.

80

chi gham azīn ki baṭ-e bādah sust parvāz ast
ki dar giriftan-e rang-e parīdah shahbāz ast

bajāyē bakhyah zanad baski khandah bar zakhmam
hamīshah sūzan-e bī raḥam rā dahān bāz ast

81

taubah az may na kunam dar pīrī
may kashī dar shab-e mahtāb khush ast

tā bakay tishnaye khūnam bāshad
tīgh rā bidihī āb khush ast

80

Why grieve if wine's
water bird is slow to take off?
In capturing the colour that has fled
it becomes a royal falcon.

Not in stitching but mocking
at my wounds does it delight.
The cruel needle ever keeps
its mouth wide open.

81

In old age too, I shall not
repent of drinking wine.
A draught of vintage is
delightful on moonlit nights.[52]

How long will it thirst
for my blood?
Better that the sword's
thirst be quenched.

82

pīsh-e śayyād ravam bāl fishān az sar-e shauq
gar bidānam gharẑash rīkhtan-e bāl-e man ast

hīchgah lab nakunad bāz ba dushnām-e raqīb
man ba tang āmadam az yār ki pur bīdahan ast

83

az kināram dukhtar-e raz kard tā pahlū tihī
kār-e man aknūn Ghanī bā ṭifl-e ashk uftādah ast

84

ahl-e dil az tark-e khwāb sair-e falak mīkunand
'Isā-e vaqt-e khud ast har ki shabī zindah dāsht

82

In joy I would rush to
the fowler with open arms.
If only I knew he would
strip me of my wings.

Not once did she open her
mouth to curse the rival.
I am fed up of a love
so tight-lipped.[53]

83

Since the daughter of vine
has slipped from my embrace,
Ghani, I am left to deal
with the child of tears.[54]

84

Sacrificing sleep, living
souls traverse the skies.
He who keeps vigil during
nights is the Jesus of his age.[55]

85

shakl-e gardūn girah u śūrat-e akhtar girah ast
kāram az anjum-u-aflāk girah dar girah ast

86

dil baski mukaddar zi jahān-e guźrān ast
chun shīshaye sāʿat nafasam rīg-e rawān ast

87

zi shauqat chāk-e jīb-e ghunchahā tā dāman uftādast
biyā kaz intiźarat gul ba chashm-e gulshan uftādast

88

marā ba khānah sifālī zi bīnavāyī nīst
khusham ki dar kaf-e man kāsaye gadāyi nīst

85

The firmament and my fortune-star
both resemble a knot.
My fortune is thus entangled
in a knot within a knot.

86

Fleeting time sullies my heart
such that my breath flows
Like sand in the hourglass.

87

Down to hems have the rosebuds
rent their garments in your love.
Come, pining for you the garden's
eye has turned sore!

88

Not even an earthen bowl has
poverty spared in my abode.
I am glad there is no begging bowl
for my hand to hold!

89

Kashmīr az śabāhat raushangar-e jamāl ast
ḥusn-e siyāh ānja gar hast khāl khāl ast

90

mārā ba ghair dāgh-e jigar dar ayāgh nīst
chūn lālah durd-e sāghar-e mā ghair-e dāgh nīst

91

az mauj kujā bastah shavad rakhnaye girdāb
bar zakhm-e dilam bakhyah zadan naqsh bar āb ast

92

dar har namāz dast ba zānū chirā zanad
zāhid agar zi kardah pashīmān nagashtah ast

89

Kashmir's beauty sparkles
through its fairness.
Black beauty here, if any,
is as rare as a mole.

90

My earthen cup holds nothing
but a branded heart.
Like the tulip, the dregs in my
goblet are but a stain.

91

How can the wave mend
the fissure of the whirlpool?
An engraving upon water is
the dressing on my heart's wound.

92

In every prayer he places
his hands on his knees.
Does the ascetic regret his act?

93

sa'īye muflis kay bajāye mīrasad
ādam-e bī barg tīr-e bī par ast

94

dar mauj khīz-e giryaye man tā kunad shinā
daryā ba pusht-e khwīsh kadūye ḥabāb bast

95

baski ba tarīqaye shabhāye gham khū kardah būd
'āqibat parvānah dar pāye chirāgh ārām yāft

96

Ghanī zīr-e zamīn ahl-e fanā rā
buvad 'aishī ki bar rūye zamīn nīst

93

How can a poor man's striving
attain its end?
A stripped man is a tuftless arrow.

94

That it may swim across
the torrent of my tears,
The sea set afloat a gourd
of bubble on its back.

95

Accustomed to the dark
nights of grief,
The moth finally finds peace
at the lamp's feet.

96

For those who embrace
self-extinction, Ghani,
Await beneath the earth joys
unknown to those above it.

97

az sharm-e zuhd-e khushk ba maikhānah tar shud ast
gar baʿd azīn vuẑū nakunad pārsā rawāst

98

chashm-e nargis pīsh-e chashmat kay tavānad shud safīd
chashm-e tū har chand bīmār ast ammā zard nīst

99

ʿāqil ān bih ki buvad chashm barāh-e murdan
az paye bī basrān khwāb bih az bīdāri ast

100

bād-e ṣabā ba gulshan-e ĥusn-e tū rāh na yāft
ān ghunchaye dahān ba nasīm-e sukhan shiguft

97

Remorseful of his arid self-denial,
he is now drenched in the tavern.
It befits the devout not to wash
himself from now.

98

In your presence how can the
narcissus's eye attain whiteness?
Howsoever sick, your eye is never pale.

99

Wise is the man awaiting death.
For the sightless sleep fares
better than wakefulness.

100

The morning breeze has no access
to the garden of your beauty.
Only the zephyr of speech makes
the bud-like mouth bloom.

101

muĥtasib khwāhi kunī bīkār gar khammār rā
shīshah hāye dānaye angūr mībāyad shikast

102

kashtiye man chūn buvad aiman darīn baĥr az shikast
langar az sargashtgī sang-e falākhun gashtah ast

103

ĥusnī ki safīd ast nadārad mazah chandān
hamrang-e namak hast u līkin namkīn nīst

104

zi sail-e ashk-e mā dar 'ālam-e khāk
ghubarī gar buvad dar khāṭir-e māst

101

Prohibitor! Want to make the
wine maker redundant?
Better that you crush the
grape cups.[56]

102

When my boat escaped wreckage
from the midst of the sea,
The harbour rose in tumult
like a catapult's stone.

103

Fair beauty is tasteless:
Salt-coloured, not salty.

104

In the dust-laden world
the flood of my tears
Swept away all save the
dust of my thoughts.

105

dar simā'-e naghmah chāk az baski shud pairāhanam
dar libāsam ghair-e tār-e chand chūn ṭanbūr nīst

106

kas namīgīrad khabar yakdam zi ĥālam dar khumār
bī kasam tā nashaye may az sar-e man raftah ast

107

dast az jān shustan āsānast dar shabhāye hijr
mītavān chūn sham' khūn-e khud barang-e āb rīkht

108

khalq sar gardān hamah az qaht-e āb-u-dānah and
har kirā dīdam ghair az āsiyā dar gardish ast

105

The enrapturing song tore
my robe to shreds.
Like a lute I had
but a few strings on.

106

No one inquired after me
in the state of a hangover.
Helpless am I since
ebriety has passed.

107

Washing hands of life is easy
in the nights of separation.
Like the candle one can shed
one's blood soundlessly.

108

Scarcity makes men wanderers.
All but the millstone are on the move.

109

chunān zi sair-e chaman dil shikastah am bī may
ki sabzah dar tah-e pāyam chū rīzaye mīnāst

110

kunad dar har qadam faryād khalkhāl
ki ĥusn-e gul rukhān pā dar rikāb ast

111

rasad ba gūsh-e man āwāz har dam az lab-e gūr
biyā ki khāk zi shauq-e tū chashm dar rāh ast

112

imshab ki az sūz-e darūn nabẑam chū tār-e sham'būd
ta'vīz bar bāzūye man hamchūn par-e parvānah sūkht

109

When sober, a stroll in the
garden was heart-shattering.
The grass under my feet was
like bits of broken flask.

110

With every step the
anklet cries out:
'Beauty, O fair ones,
has her feet in the stirrup.'

111

From the grave I hear
a call every moment:
'Come, the dust's eye
pines for you.'

112

Tonight the fire within made
my pulse flicker like a candle,
And the amulet on my arm
burnt up like a moth's wing.

113

bugzar az khwīsh chū bīnī dahān-e yār Ghanī
dil ba hastī chi nihī rāh-e ʿadam darpīsh ast

114

bī riyāżat nashavad nashaye ʿirfān ĥāsil
tā kadū khushk na gardīd maye nāb na yāft

115

har ĥalqaye zulf-e tū dahānī shudah az shauq
bugzār ki yakbār bibūsīd kaf-e pāyat

116

tāqat-e barkhāstan chūn gard-e namnākam namānd
khalq pindārad ki may khurdast u mast uftādah ast

113

Ghani, as you behold love's
lips, pass beyond yourself.
Why set your heart on life when
the road to eternity beckons?[57]

114

Without discipline the ebriety
of gnosis cannot be tasted.
No wine is ready till the gourd dries up.

115

Longing has curled your
tresses into round lips.
Permit them to cascade
and kiss your feet once.

116

Like moist dust I've no strength to rise.
They think I'm supine because I'm drunk.

117

taghāful-e tū marā khush numāyad az luṭfat
ki īn ba har kas u ān khāsah az barāye man ast

118

chu sar ba pāye tū sūdam zi dard-e sar rastam
hināye pāye tū am kard kār-e śandal-e surkh

119

lab-e laʿlat chū muqābil ba maye nāb shavad
sāghar-e bādah zi khijlat chū ḥabāb āb shavad

bakht-e shūram shudah az baski gulūgīr Ghanī
gar chakānī ba labam shīr namak āb shavad

117

Your indifference delights me
more than your concern.
For it is reserved for me while
others partake of the latter.

118

Bruising my head against your
feet relieved me of pain.
The henna of your feet
acted like a red balm.

119

When the ruby wine came
face-to-face with your lips,
Like a burst bubble, every
goblet turned to water out of shame.

Bitter luck has tied itself
around my neck, Ghani.
If you sprinkle milk on my lips,
it will turn brackish.

120

shukrānaye tīrī ki guzar az dil-u-jān kard
az daur-e saram sajdah ba miĥrāb-e kamān kard

bīzāram azān 'umr ki vābastaye rūzī ast
chūn śubĥ marā dīdan-e nān sīr zi jān kard

tā āb-e rukh-e muĥtasib-e shehar narīzad
mā kashtiye may rā natavānīm ravān kard

har chand Ghanī hamchū nigīn khānah nishīn ast
nāmash zi dar-e bastah bar āyad chi tavān kard

121

zi sharm-e chashm-e tū bādām khushk tar gardad
maye rasīdah chū bīnad lab-e tū bar gardad

120

Her arrow went past my soul and heart;
thank God a hundred times!
And circling my head knelt again
in the bow's arch.

At dawn a glimpse of bread
makes me forget my soul.
I am distressed by a life
so hinged on sustenance.

Until the sweat of honour
drains off the town's prohibitor
I cannot set sail my wine boat.

Howsoever Ghani stays put
in his abode like a seal,
His name slips through the
closed door: what is he to do?

121

Shamed by your eye,
the almond shall turn drier.
And faced with your lips
the vintage wine shall turn bland.

zi khud numāyī bugżar ba mausim-e pīrī
chū abrah kuhnah shavad bih ki astar gardad

ba bazm-e bādah żarūr ast gardish-e jāmī
chū nīst sāghar-e may kāsahāye sar gardad

122

garmiye az dil-e sakht-e tū nadīdam hargiz
bāvaram nīst ki ātash ʿalam az sang shavad

123

muḥtasib bar dar-e maykhāna nishastan dārad
shīshaye dānaye angūr shikastan dārad

har dam az gūshaye khāṭir sar jastan dārad
maʾnaye tāzah ghazālīst ki bastan dārad

In the season of old age
give up self-display.
The worn-out cloth serves
better as an inner lining.

In the wine assembly you need
to keep cups in motion.
If not cups, cup-shaped heads will do.

122

No warmth did I find
in your stony heart.
Who says that a stone
hides a spark?

123

The prohibitor sits in
the tavern's doorway,
Smashing the cups of grapes.

Every moment it seeks to slip
from the mind's nook.
Fresh poetic meaning is a gazelle
to be captured.[58]

zang az dil nabarad dar shab-e hijrat mahtāb
bī rukhat āyīnaye māh shikastan dārad

naqsh-e pāyam zi rah-e khāk nishīnī gūyad
ki bahar jā ki nishānand nishastan dārad

124

ān chashm-e mast bādah kashī rā chū ʿām kard
nargis zarī ki dāsht hamah śarf-e jām kard

tā būd guftgū sukhanam nātamām būd
nāzam ba khāmshī ki sukhan rā tamām kard

125

andīshah nadāshtam az dil ki khūn shavad
dāgham azīn ki dāgh-e tū az dil birūn shavad

In the night of parting, the glowing
moon cannot cleanse the heart's rust.
Deprived of your visage, its mirror
seeks to smash itself.

Set into dust,
my footprints whisper:
'Let us be seated wherever
they make us sit.'

124

When that drunken eye
made drinking universal,
The narcissus spent all its
capital on the cup.

My speech remained unfinished
as long as I spoke.
Proud that I accomplished
it with my silence.

125

I fear not that my heart
might be crushed to blood.
But I am anguished that your
scar might fade away from it.

gūyad zabān-e shīshah nihāni ba gūsh-e jām
har kas ki sar kashad ba jahān sar nigūn shavad

chūn panbah khushk gasht Ghanī maghẑ dar saram
zībad agar fatīlaye dāgh-e junūn shavad

126

bar zabān qāni' agar ḣarf-e lab-e nān gīrad
zūd az sharam zabān dar tah-e dandān gīrad

tā ghubārī zi sar-e kūye tū rūbad khurshīd
nūr dar dīdaye u śūrat-e miĵgān gīrad

dar dām-e śubḣ Ghanī pīr-e falak mīgūyad
ki qaẑā nān dihad ān laḣẑah ki dandān gīrad

The flask's hidden tongue
whispers into the cup's ear:
'He who raises his head high
shall be humbled.'

Since my brain has dried up
like a cotton ball inside my head
It can serve as a gauze
for the scar of my frenzy.

126

If the austere one's tongue
ever utters the word 'bread',
Soon will shame make him
bite it between his teeth.

That the sun may wipe
away dust from your street,
Its eye emits rays in the
form of eyelashes.

At the break of dawn, Ghani,
the old Saturn whispers thus:
'Fate provides bread the moment
it snatches the teeth.'[59]

127

ba ruz-e hijr kay sair-e gulistānam havas dāram
ki gulban bī gul-e rūye tū dar chashmam qafas bāshad

bidih az sabzaye khaṭ murgh-e dil rā khaṭ-e āzādī
chū maghẑ-e pistah tā kay ṭūṭiye mā dar qafas bāshad

128

hāsid az kardaye khud gasht pashīmān ki ba zūr
bar zamīn zad sukhan-e man va ba aflāk rasīd

129

Manṡūr bār bast zi dunyā u dār mānd
parvāz kard gul zi gulistān u khār mānd

127

Parted from you, my heart
desires not the garden.
Without your rosy cheek,
the rosebush is a prison.

For the heart's bird, pass a writ
of freedom from that greenish down.
How long will our parrot be caged
like a pistachio's kernel?

128

The jealous rival regretted his act,
for when with vehemence
He dashed my verse to the ground,
it reached the skies.

129

Mansur bore himself away
and left the gibbet behind.
Mark, the rose is fled but
the thorn abides its place.[60]

hamchūn sapīdayī ki buvad gird-e mardumak
tā dīd panbah dāgh-e marā bar kinār mānd

bugzasht 'umr u mūye safīdī ba jā gużasht
khākistrī zi qāflaye yādgār mānd

130

surmah uftād zi chashm-e tū u ruswā gardīd
chūn siyah mast ki az rauzan-e maykhāna futad

sham'-e āham ki kunad bazm-e falak rā raushan
akhtar-e sūkhtah am chūn par-e parvānah futad

kūdkān sang ba kaf bar sar-e rāhand Ghanī
khwāham īn qur'ah ba nām-e man-e dīvānah zadand

Like the whiteness which
surrounds the eye's pupil,
To watch my scar the
white dressing stands aloof.

Life itself has passed and left
behind a few white strands.
The ashes left behind tell
of the caravan past.

130

Falling from your eyes, the
kohl fell into disgrace.
Like a drunken sot who falls
down the tavern's window.

The candle of my sighs
irradiates the sky's assembly.
I am a burnt star fallen
like the moth's wing.

Stones in hands, street urchins
wait in ambush, Ghani.
How I wish the lot falls
to this madman's name!

131

riyāẑ-e ĥusnash az khūn-e dil-e man tāzah mīgardad
zi rūyam mīparad rang u ba rūyash ghāzah mīgardad

chū girdābam man-e mahjūr ba jām-e tihī sarkhush
labam paivastah bar gird-e lab-e khamyāzah mīgardad

132

faiz-e sukhan ba mard-e sukhangū namī rasad
az nāfah būye mushk ba āhū namī rasad

ẕāhid ba yār tuhmat-e śahba kashī makun
paidāst īnki may ba lab-e u namī rasad

131

My heart's blood gives freshness
to her beauty's garden.
The sheen flees from my
face to adorn her cheeks.

Forlorn, yet drunk on an
empty cup like a whirlpool.
My lips remain glued to
those open lips.

132

Seldom does the poet derive
benefit from his verse.
The musk's fragrance always
eludes the deer.

Blame her not, O ascetic, for
sipping the draught of wine.
There's not a sign that it
has kissed her lips.

133

āyad az tār-e nafas ṭā'ir-e ma'nī dar dām
ay ḥarīfān qafas-e gūsh muhayyā dārīd

134

nayaftad partavī bar māh gar az sham'-e rukhsārash
ba gardish hālah hamchūn shu'la-e javvālah mīgardad

chasān az hamdamān dāram nihān dard-e dil khud rā
ki hamchūn nay nafas dar sīnaye man nālah mīgardad

135

chāk-e pairāhan-e Yūsuf nabvad bī ma'nī
khandah bar pākiye dāmān-e Zuleikhā dārad

133

The bird of meaning is ensnared
with the string of breath.
Friends, be ready to
cage it in your ears.

134

If the candle of her face
sheds no light on the moon,
Its halo will only swirl like
a circling flame.

I hid my heart's torment
from my friends and now,
Like the flute's lament, my
breath rages within my breast.

135

The torn shirt of Yusuf,
full of meaning,
Mocks at Zuleikha's
mantle of chastity.[61]

baski dar gūshaye ʿuzlat chū Ghanī dil bastam
har ki shud gūshah nishīn dar dil-e man jā dārad

136

nihālī rā ki dihqān kand az jā kay ṣamar gīrad
namī khwāham ki mā rā āsmān az khāk bar gīrad

137

az sālikān-e raftah nishāni ba jā namānd
bar āb har ki raft azū naqsh-e pā namānd

138

tā chashm dūkhtam zi jahān bīnisham farūz
sūzan barāye dīdaye man mīl-e surmah būd

Like Ghani, a solitary
corner so much I love,
That every recluse finds
a place in my heart.

136

Unearthed by the farmer,
can the sapling bear fruit?
Let me, O heavens,
remain inearthed!

137

No sign of the passers-by
can one discern.
The traveller on water
leaves no trace.

138

Stitching the eye from
the world, I gained in vision.
For me the needle became
the kohl stick.

139

dūsh bī may dil zi sair-e bāgh dar āzār būd
kāsaye sar hamchū nargis bar tan-e mā bār būd

140

kasī āvārah tā kay dar dayār-e khwīshtan bāshad
chū rīg-e shīshaye sā'at musāfir dar vatan bāshad

141

tabkhālah ki jā bar lab-e ān hūsh rubā kard
may rīkht ba jām-e khud u khūn dar dil-e mā kard

142

gard-e dāman-e taghāful naravad az yādam
īn ghubārīst ki dar khāṭir-e mā mīgardad

139

Without ebriety, yesterday I
strolled in the garden distressed.
Like the narcissus, my head
weighed upon my body.

140

How long can one
wander in one's abode,
And like sand in an
hourglass be a traveller at home?

141

The blister that has made a place
on the lips of the mesmerizer,
Pours wine into its cup,
leaving my heart bleeding.

142

The marks of apathy have
stuck to my memory.
They are the dust that still
roams through my mind.

143

kibr dar silsilaye bādah kashān kam bāshad
tāk har chand ki bī bar buvad kham bāshad

144

chūn ba sair-e chaman ān dilbar-e ṭannāz āyad
rang-e gul bīshtar az būy ba parvāz āyad

145

khush ān zamān ki tīrash az shast jastah bāshad
dar pahlūyam chū tarkash tā par nishashtah bāshad

146

buvad dar iẑtirāb az ahl-e ʿālam har ki kāmil shud
tapīdan darmiyān-e jumlah aʿẑā qismat-e dil shud

143

Pride is not the way of the wine lovers.
Fruitless, yet the vine remains bent.

144

When that coquettish one
strolled into the garden,
Faster than fragrance fled
the colour of the rose.

145

Happy the hour when the arrow
flies from her bow,
And, as in a quiver, rests in
my side spreading its feathers.

146

Only the perfect
know restlessness.
Only the heart among
organs is fated to throb.

147

naṣīb-e mā zi bāgh-e āfrīnish mīvaye gham shud
nihālī rā ki parvardīm ākhir nakhl-e mātam shud

148

az charkh bī maẓallat ĥājat ravā nagardad
tā ābru na rīzī īn āsiyā nagardad

149

dīdah am az dīdan-e vaẑ'-e jahān ranjūr shud
zakhm-e chashmam rā safīdī marĥam-e kāfūr shud

150

chū sheikh-e shehar turā dīd dar namāz uftad
damī agarchi ba pā istād bāz uftad

147

From the garden of creation,
we only got the fruit of grief.
The sapling we nurtured grew
into a tree of mourning.

148

The sky provides not
till you know disgrace.
This millstone moves not
till you shed your brow's sweat.

149

The spectacle of the
world wounds my eye.
Like camphor, whiteness
becomes its balm.[62]

150

As the sheikh caught a glimpse of you,
he fell in his namaz.
He rose for a moment and
fell down again.

151

ān āftāb-e tābān chūn bī naqāb gardad
dar chāh māh-e Kan'ān az sharm āb gardad

152

sipand āsā agar pīsh-e khudam dar ātash andāzad
azān bihtar ki dūr az khwīsh chūn chashm-e badam sāzad

153

māh andākht sipar chūn ṭaraf-e rūye tū shud
kāst az ghairat u ham chashm ba abrūye tū shud

154

nabvad zi shauq-e bāl-e humā iẑtirāb-e man
chashmam zi ishtiyāq-e par-e kāh mī parad

151

When the bright sun
removed its veil,
In the well the moon of Canaan
was drenched with shame.[63]

152

Better that like rue
she cast me into flames,
And not away like the evil eye.

153

Up against your visage,
the moon cast off its shield.
Consumed by shame,
it emulated your eyebrow.

154

I'm not in anguish pining
for the huma's wing.
My eye has become restive
yearning for a blade of grass.[64]

155

farīb-e niʿmat-e shāhān makhūr ki az faghfūr
śadāye kāsaye khālī ba gūsh mī āyad

156

kār-e kasī bar ār ki khud ham rasī ba kār
chūn gul nishān shavad par-e bulbul ba tīr band

157

mānand-e āftāb ki raushan shavad ba śubĥ
dāgh-e dilam zi marham-e kāfūr tāzah shud

158

tā harf-e may parastān guftī shunīd zāhid
hushyār bāsh īnjā dīvār gūsh dārad

155

Let not the emperors' riches
beguile you, for their porcelain
Sends out to the ears a hollow sound.

156

Strive to fulfil others' tasks,
if you desire yours fulfilled.
You desire the rose? Make your arrow's
tuft out of the nightingale's feathers.

157

Like the sun that shines
when it is morn,
The balm of camphor
brands my heart afresh.

158

About to speak against
drinkers, the ascetic heard:
'Beware, walls too have ears here.'

159

dilam rā khāl-e ū duzdīd u dar gard-e khaṭash jūyam
ki māl-e burdah rā duzdān nihān dar khāk misāzand

160

aṣar bar ʿaks bakhshad saʿye man az ṭalʿi vājĝūn
zi faryād-e sipandam chashm-e bad az khwāb bar khīzad

161

śad maikadah rā rang ba har gūshah tavān rīkht
zān surmah ki az chashm-e siyāh-e mast-e tū uftād

162

ba kārgāh-e tamāshā naqāb-e rūye turā
zi tār-e sha'sha'-e āftāb mī bāfand

159

Her mole stole my heart
and I search it in her dusty down.
For thieves hide stolen wealth
under the earth.

160

Thanks to my inverted fortune,
my efforts have a reverse effect.
The laments of my burning rue
awaken the evil eye.[65]

161

A hundred taverns are
drenched in blackness
By the kohl that falls from
your drunken black eyes.

162

In the world of wonders,
the veil of your face
Is woven from the
glittering beams of the sun.

163

murīd-e Khizr tavān shud ki ba ḣayāt-e abad
tan az ḣijāb ba iźhār-e zindagī na dihad

164

kilk-e man chūn khāmaye mū rīshah rīshah shud zi mashq
līk azīn dāgham ki khaṭam śūratī paidā nakard

165

kārvān bugzasht u man az kāhlī māndam ba rāh
bahr-e khwāb-e pāyam āvāz-e jaras afsānah shud

166

zi shiʿr-e man dīgrān kāmyāb u man maḣrūm
zabān chū gūsh kujā laźźat-e sukhan yābad

163

You can become Khizr's
disciple if all your life
You give not yourself
to self-display.[66]

164

Practising, my pen came apart in
shreds like the painter's brush.
How sad it could not draw a single portrait!

165

The caravan left and my indolence
left me stranded behind.
Its bell was a tale that sent
my feet to sleep.

166

My poems delight others
and leave me wanting.
How can the tongue match
the ear in relishing speech?

167

sakht dilbastagī dāsht ba bālam śayyād
tā nashud bālish-e u pur zi param khwāb nakard

168

nīst ĥusn-e bī baqā shāyistaye dil bastgī
bā chirāgh-e barq yak parvānah hamrāhi na kard

169

hīch kas bar ĥāl-e mā raĥmī na kard
tishnah lab murdīm u chashmī tar na shud

170

yārān burdand shiʿr-e mārā
afsūs ki nām-e ma na burdand

171

mī farastad ba pidar pairahan-e khālī rā
Yūsuf az daulat-e ĥusn īnhama khud rā gum kard

167

So enamoured of my wings
is the fowler's heart that
His eye catches sleep only
on the pillow of my feathers.

168

Fleeting beauty is unworthy of love.
The lamp of lightning's flash attracts
no moth.

169

None took pity on me.
I died and no eye became moist.

170

Friends took my verses.
Pity, they took not my name.

171

He sent his father an empty robe:
Thus had Yusuf lost himself to
the beauty's glamour.[67]

172

jazāye śidq-e mukāfāt dar jahān īn bas
ki 'umr-e qātil-e parvānah tā sahar na kashīd

173

tā kay tū bar zamīn ravī u māh bar āsmān
ṭarĥ-e jahān khush ast ki zīr-u-zabar shavad

174

tan ba murdan nih Ghanī chūn qāmatat gardīd kham
bahr-e īn khātam nigīnī nīst juz sang-e mazār

175

dar ṭalab-e būye tū ay gul 'iżār
āblah pāy ast zi shabnam bahār

172

The truth of retribution
in the world is this alone:
'The life of the moth's killer
does not extend beyond dawn.'

173

How long will you walk the earth
and the moon the sky?
Better that the worlds
turn upside down!

174

Ghani, give up your body
bent with age to death.
Except the gravestone
no gem will fit this ring.

175

To catch your fragrance,
O rosy-cheeked one,
Spring has its feet
blistered due to dew.

176

dar pāye nihālī chū marā mast bigīrī
chūn khūshah am ay muĥtasib az tāk biyāvīz

177

Ghanī chū sāyaye murgh-e parindah dar shauq
agar ba khāk biyaftam nayaftam az parvāz

178

saʿiye rūzī bar namī dārad marā az jāye khwīsh
ābrū chūn shamʿ mī rīzam valī dar pāye khwīsh

179

sūz-e dilī ki dāram az giryah kam na gardad
chūn shamʿ āb-e chashmam bāshad ghiżāye man

176

If you catch me drunk
at the sapling's feet,
Hang me, O prohibitor,
like a bunch from the vine.

177

Ghani, like the shadow of the bird
flying in the course of love,
Falling into the dust will not
disrupt my flight.

178

The search for sustenance moves
me not from my place.
Like the candle, I shed my
honour only at my feet.

179

Tears do not lessen my heart's anguish.
Like the candle my tears feed the flame.

180

kas ba'd-e marg giryah ba ĥālam namī kunad
dar zindagī chū sham' bigīram ba ĥāl-e khwīsh

181

kujā gardad muyassar ni'mat-e dīdār chashmī rā
ki mijˆgān baham chaspīdah az shīrīniye khwābash

182

raushan zi man jahān u man az bakht-e tīrah dāgh
kay sāyaye chirāg shavad maĥav az chirāgh

183

juz maye bī ghash makhūr bahr-e śafāye dimāgh
raughan agar śāf nīst tīrah farūzad chirāgh

180

None shed a tear
for me after death.
I alone bemoaned my
lot like the candle when alive.

181

How can the eyes relish
the delight of vision,
When the eyelashes are
glued together by her sweet dream?

182

I illuminate the world,
myself darkened by ill luck.
How can the lamp rid itself
of its shadow?

183

Save pure wine sip nothing
to cleanse your spirit.
Oil that is impure robs the
lamp of its glow.

184

hargiz sukhan-e zāhid-e dil-e murdah na gūyam
tarsam ki labam hamchū lab-e gūr shavad khushk

zāhid buru az bāgh ki chūn muhraye tasbîh
az chashm-e badat dānaye angūr shavad khushk

185

sarv dar faśl-e khizān mānad bahāl
rāstī rā nabvad bīm-e zawāl

186

nīst shuhrat ṭalab ānkas ki kamālī dārad
hargiz angusht numā badr nabāshad chū hilāl

184

The ascetic—dead of heart; his words
I shall never utter.
For I fear my lip will turn dry
as a grave's mouth.

Leave the garden, ascetic,
for your evil eye
Might turn the grapes
dry as the rosary's beads.

185

The cypress remains
intact even in autumn.
Uprightness fears no decline.

186

An accomplished man
hankers not after fame.
The crescent, and not the full moon,
needs to be pointed at.[68]

187

nishān-e harzih gardī żāhir ast az ṭarz-e raftāram
buvad sargashtgī paidā zi naqsh-e pā chū pargāram

bar angushtash ba pīcham rishtaye bārīk tar az mū
dihad tā ān taghāful pīshah rā yād az tan-e zāram

darīn gulshan nabāshad ṭūṭiye shīrīn sukhan chūn man
ba kār-e naishkar śad ʿuqdah afgandast minqāram

Ghanī az gulkhan-e gītī ba akhgar mīzanam pahlū
ki az sūz-e darūn khākistarī shud rang-e rukhsāram

188

dar hamraham gham-e vatan ast
gul-e bā khār chīdah rā mānam

187

My meandering steps
point to my wanderlust.
My footprints, like the compass,
tell of my bewilderment.

On her finger I shall wind
a thread finer than hair.
Perhaps it will remind that
heedless one of my frail frame.

No bird in this garden
sings as sweetly as I.
Pecking on sugar, I cast blight
on the sugar seller's trade.

The world is a bonfire, Ghani,
and I am like an ember.
My cheeks are ashen while
fire smoulders within.

188

Grief for my land accompanies
me wherever I go.
I am a rose plucked
along with the thorn.

khandah am dar kamīn-e parvāz ast
kabak-e shahbāz dīdah ra mānam

rīkht khūnam ba rang-e āb-e siphar
rag-e tāk-e burīdah mānam

bī tū bar farsh-e gul zi bītabī
murgh-e dar khūn tapīdah rā mānam

189

āsūdgī ba gūshaye hastī nadīdah īm
jān dādah īm u kunj-e mazārī kharīdah īm

chūn sham' buvad manzil-e mā zīr-e pāye man
az pā nishastah īm u ba manzil rasīdah īm

The smile on my face is
about to take flight,
Like a partridge that has
sighted a falcon.

As water pours down the skies
blood drips from me.
I am a vein of the vine slit open.

Pining for you on the
rose-decked floor,
I am a bird wallowing
in its own blood.

189

Peace was never my lot in life.
For a corner of the graveyard
I paid with my life.

Like the candle my destination
lay beneath my feet.
I sat and reached the journey's end.

190

chūn sham'-e shab ba giryah u āhi nishastah īm
vaqt-e śahar ba rūz-e siyāhī nishastah īm

191

kardah zi jahān shugl-e sukhan gūshah nishīnam
tā khāmah musāfir shudah man khānah nishīnam

192

tā zi bazm-e viśāl-e ū dūram
zindah am līk zindah dar gūram

193

yār tā qatl chunīn bāshad agar hamrāham
safar-e mulk-e 'adam rā zi khudā mīkhwāham

190

Like a candle my night was spent
sobbing and sighing.
And the dawn promised
another dark day.

191

My vocation has made
a recluse of me.
I have sat home that
my pen may travel.

192

As long as I am away
from her presence,
I live but a living death.

193

If my love accompanies
me to my execution,
A journey to the other world
I shall seek from God.

194

jalwaye ĥusn-e turā āwarad marā bar sar-e fikr
tū ĥinā bastī u man māʿnaye rangīn bastam

195

az fikr tā sukhan nashavad qābil-e raqam
mānand-e khāmah sar zi girīban namī kasham

196

jān ba lab az ẑʿuf natāvanad rasīd
mā ba zūr-e nātavāni zindah am

197

mīkunad pahlū tihī az bī navāyān āsmān
dar baghal hargiz na gīrad tīr-e bī par rā kamān

194

The spectacle of your beauty
sets me reflecting.
Composing colourful themes
keeps up with your self-adorning.

195

Until reflection has made the verse
fit for composition,
Like the pen, my head remains
sunk in my shirt's collar.

196

So enfeebled that life
struggles to reach my lips,
The strength of my infirmity
keeps me alive.

197

The sky too shuns
the hapless ones.
And the bow never
holds a tuftless arrow.

just-u-jū az bahr-e rūzi bā'iṣ-e sharmandgīst
zīn khajālat āsiyā angusht dārad dar dahān

kāmyāb az jām-e vaslat ghair u man az rashk-e dāgh
āb mīgardad marā dar dīdah ū rā dar dahān

jam' kardam musht-e khāshākī ki sūzam khwīsh rā
gul gumān dārad ki bandam āshiyān dar gulistān

bā sabuksārān Ghanī paivastah hamrāhi guzīn
rāh ba sāhil mī barad kashtī ba zūr-e bādbān

198

gar chirāgh-e ĥusn-e ū raushan shavad dar anjuman
dar dahān angusht-e sham' az sharm mīgīrad lagan

Remorse is the lot of those
wandering for a living.
The millstone bites its
finger out of shame.[69]

The bliss of union is the rival's lot,
the scar of envy mine.
His mouth a well of wine,
my eye that of tears.

To set myself ablaze, I
gathered a handful of straw.
And the rose thought I
intended a nest in the garden.

While journeying, Ghani,
seek the company of the light ones.
It's the frail sail which sees the boat through.

198

If the lamp of her beauty
shines in the gathering,
A vessel dripping with
shame will the candle be.

kay zanad pahlū ba man Majnūn ki dar khāk-e junūn
sang-e ṭiflān shud marā chūn ustkhwān juzv-e badan

gar falak kār-e turā barham zanad az jā marū
jāmah rā khayyāṭ sāzad qatʿ bahr-e dūkhtan

dar muḥabbat ʿishqbāzān mīkunand imdād ham
sang-e ṭiflān bahr-e Majnūn mītarāshad Kūhkan

khāk pīzi tā ba kay chūn shīshaye sāʿat Ghanī
naqd-e auqātī ki gum shud bāz natavān yāftan

199

biyā sāqī shabistān-e marā imshab munavvar kun
zi rauzan tā bar āyad āftābam may ba sāghar kun

In frenzy, Majnun is
no match for me.
Not bones but the urchins' stones
constitute my frame.

Grieve not if the heavens
thwart your plans.
The tailor rips the cloth
to sew it back.

In love's ordeal lovers come
to each other's rescue.
For Majnun's sake Kuhkan
furnishes the urchins with stones.[70]

For how long, Ghani, will you
sift sand like the hourglass?
The wealth of time once lost
can never be regained.

199

Come, Saki, illuminate
my dark chamber tonight.
Pour wine into my cup that
the sun may shine in my abode.

gul-e bī khār-e gulzār-e khamūshī chīdanī dārad
zabān-e guftgū rā hamchū nā farmān pas-e sar kun

Ghanī faśl-e bahār āmad gul-e ʿaishī tavān chīdan
birūn āvar chū nargis zar zi khāk u sarf-e sāghar kun

200

dīdam ki nuktah sanjān duzdand shiʿr-e mardum
man nīz shiʿr-e khud rā duzdīdam az ḣarīfān

zi shiʿr-e man shudah pushīdah faẑl-u-dānish-e man
chū mīvaye ki bimānad ba zīr-e barg nihān

201

az baski shiʿr guftan shud mubtażil darīn ʿahd
lab bastan ast aknūn maẑmūn-e tāzah bastan

172

The thornless rose of the garden
of silence is worth picking.
Lay off the prattling tongue
like an unruly slave.

Ghani, the rose of life's bounty
awaits picking in the spring.
Like the narcissus bring out gold
from the earth and spend it on the cup.

200

I saw that poets steal
each other's verses.
I am still retrieving
those stolen by my peers.

My poetry has concealed
my knowledge and wisdom,
Like the fruit which is hidden
by the leaves of the tree.

201

Saying verse has fallen into
such disgrace today,
Sealing one's lips is the only
novel theme to be composed.

202

ba gulshan bī tū abr-e dīdaye mā rīkht bārānī
ki gardīd āshiyān-e 'andlībān chashm-e giryānī

shavad dar kunj-e faqr az rakhnahāye būrya raushan
ki dard-e khāksārān rā nabāshad hīch darmānī

biyā dar dīdah am binishīn agar āb-e ravān khwāhī
ki az chashm-e taram jūyīst har chāk-e girībānī

chi khush bālidah ast az giryah bar khud mardum-e chashmam
futādah darmiyān-e āb gūya tukhm-e raihānī

dilam chūn girdbād az kūchah gardīha ba tang āmad
ba raqś āyam chū yābam rukhśat-e sair-e gulistānī

202

In the garden of love, longing
makes my eye a rain cloud,
Turning the nests of nightingales
into drenched eyes.

In the humble corner of the poor
the rents of the mat proclaim:
'The wounds of the dust-dwellers
can be healed by no balm.'

Desire a flowing stream?
Come and sit in my eye.
For it has turned every
garment's slit into a gushing stream.

How well is my eye's pupil
nurtured by its own tears!
As if a seed of basil were cast into water.

Fed up of roaming streets,
like the whirlwind,
I will dance in joy if
allowed a stroll in the garden.

Ghanī dar faśl-e gul tā kay ba kunj-e khānah binishīnī
sarī chūn khār bālā kun zi dīvār-e gulistānī

203

yār dar chashm-e man u raushan azū anjumī
ū chū sham' ast darīn majlis u man chū laganī

būd sarmāye man jāmah u jāni ākhir
jān girv jāmah girv kardah kharīdam kafanī

chi 'ajab tab'am agar da'vaye 'ijāz kunad
ki ba luṭf-e sukhanam nīst kasī rā sukhanī

baski dar daur-e jamāl-e mah-e man gasht sabuk
Yūsuf-e Miśr darāmad ba naźar pairahanī

Ghani, in the season of roses, how long
will you sit in a secluded corner?
Rise from the garden's wall,
though it be like a thorn.

203

My love sits in my eye and
illuminates the gathering.
She, a candle in the midst,
and I, the candlestick.

At last my robe and my
life proved my sole wealth.
Life in pawn, robe in pawn,
I bought myself a shroud.

What wonder if my genius
claims to be miraculous?
Matchless is the pleasure
my verse affords.

Pale beside my
revolving moon,
Yusuf of Egypt looks
no more than his shirt.

sang dar kūchah u bāzār kamī kard Ghanī
man-e Majnūn chi kunam gar nabvad Kūhkanī

204

hast az khār magar dāman-e śaĥrā khālī
ki na gardīd dil-e āblah pā khāli

ʿizzat-e shāh u gadā zīr-e zamīn yaksān ast
mīkunad khāk barāye hamah kas jā khālī

dar gham ābād-e jahān nīst baham ʿaish mudām
gasht tā jām pur az may shudah mīna khālī

205

paik-e sirishk kardam dumbāl-e bakht rāhī
kaz chashm-e man rabūdah ham khwāb ham siyāhī

Stones have disappeared from
bazaars and streets, Ghani.
Without Kuhkan what will
this hapless Majnun do?[71]

204

Though the desert's hem
is without thorns,
The heart of the blister-footed
is ever fraught with grief.

Under the earth, the king and
the beggar enjoy equal honour.
Dust makes equal room for both.

None enjoys a lasting joy
in this grief-ridden world.
As wine fills the cup,
the flask is emptied.

205

I sent the messenger of tears
after the fleeing luck.
From my eyes have fled
both sleep and sight.

yak tan darīn zamānah bī dāgh-e mātami nīst
kardīm sair-e ʿālam az māh tā ba māhī

ayman mashav zi dushman shud garchi bā tū hamrang
ātash ki khaśm-e kāh ast dārad libās-e kāhī

206

ba gūsham īn śadā az muqriye tasbīĥ mī āyad
ki śad dil muẑtarib gardad chū yak dil yābad ārāmī

shudam az ikhtilāt-e zulf-e ū mashhūr dar ʿālam
bar āvardīm ākhir az siyāhī chūn nigīn nāmī

207

dar bazm-e may nabāshad tasbīĥ rā źahūrī
nabvad sitārah hā rā dar āftāb nūrī

Not a single soul have I
seen untainted with grief,
Though I searched the world
from the sea to the sky.

Be not complacent of your enemy
though he takes on your hue.
The spark which consumes the straw
disguises as a straw.

206

From the teller of beads a whisper
reaches my ears:
'A hundred hearts lose their
peace to bring solace to one.'

The company of her tresses
made me famous throughout,
Like the seal's mark which
owes its fame to black ink.

207

In the wine assembly, the rosary
is conspicuous by its absence.
The shining sun puts all the stars to flight.

208

muddat-e shādi u gham nīst barābar ba jahān
giryaye shamʿ shabī khandaye śubĥ ast damī

209

didah dar rukhsār-e khūbān dūkhtan khush davlatast
kāshkī mijgān-e man chashmī chū sūzan dāshtī

210

har sāgharī ki būd pur az may shud u hanūz
gūyad ĥabāb-e bādah ki khālist jāye may

211

chunān nam-e man raushan ast dar Hind
ki naqsh-e nigīn dar mayān-e siyāhī

208

Grief outlasts joy in this world.
The candle cries the whole night
for a moment's laugh at dawn.

209

Sewing one's eyes to the
cheeks of fairies is delightful.
How I wish my lashes had
eyes like the needle!

210

Every goblet is brimming
with wine and still,
'There is room for more,'
cries the wine bubble.

211

My name has attained
such fame in India
As the signet ring's mark
in black ink.

Quatrains

(*Rubā'iyāt*)

1

ẑ'uf-e tū ba dil shikast paikān mā rā
śad kūh-e alam nihādah bar jān mā rā
hargiz nashunīdīm ki mū dard kunad
dard-e kamr-e tū sākht ḫairān mārā

2

kardast havāye Hind dilgīr mārā
ay bakht rasān ba bāgh-e Kashmīr mā rā
gashtam zi ḫarārat-e gharībī bītāb
az śubḫ-e vatan bidih ṭabāshīr mārā

3

tā faqr shudah muqīm-e kāshānaye mā
az gard-e amal tihī ast virānaye mā
raftan badar-e khānaye mardum 'aib ast
imrūz ki fāqah hast dar khānaye mā

4

az baski gulī nabvad dar gulshan-e mā
khāri nazad ast dast dar dāman-e mā
az chashm-e bad-e barq natarsīm ki sūkht
mānand-e sipand dānah dar khirman-e mā

Quatrains

1

Your infirmity pierces my heart with arrows
And my soul writhes under the burden of pain.
Ever heard a hair complaining of pain?
No wonder your waist's pain amazes me.

2

The scorching winds of India distress me.
O Fate, take me to the garden of Kashmir.
The heat of exile robs me of peace.
Grant me a glimpse of my land's milky dawn.

3

Since poverty has come to inhabit my dwelling
The dust of hope has fled from this desolate abode.
It is not becoming to knock on others' doors today
When hunger has arrived as a guest at mine.

4

Since no rose is left in my garden
My garment now fears not the thorn's prick.
Like wild rue I fear not lightning's evil eye
For my granary holds nothing for it to consume.

5

ay dil nakhūri farīb-e arbāb-e daghā
ghāfil nashavī zi dushman-e dūst numā
har chand ki āstīn numāyad fānūs
dar kushtan-e sham' bāshadash dast-e rasā

6

dāram dardī ki hast jānkāh marā
bāshad ay kāsh 'umr kūtāh marā
har chand ki nīst muhlik īn kūft valī
dāyim tā marg hast hamrāh marā

7

bī faham agar chashm bidūzad ba kitāb
natavānad dīd rūye ma'anī dar khwāb
kay ghaur kunand dar sukhan bī maghzān
ghavvāśiye baḣr nīst maqdūr-e ḣabāb

8

afsūs ki raft nashaye 'ahd-e shabāb
sarkhush na shudīm yak dam az bādaye nāb
az bahr-e tamāshaye jahān hamchū ḣabāb
tā vā kardīm chashm raftīm ba khwāb

5

O heart, be not beguiled by deceiving men.
Ever beware of the friend-like foe.
However much the sleeve may look like a lantern
It is ever ready to snuff out the flame.

6

Afflicted with a pain that wears me out,
Would that my life were cut short!
Not fatal, yet this gnawing pain
Will keep me company till my death.

7

A dull mind may fix its gaze on the book,
Yet meaning shall remain beyond its grasp.
The empty-headed fail to fathom the depths,
Like a hollow bubble they can never plunge the sea.

8

Alas! So swiftly did youth's ebriety pass
Before we could savour fully the ruby wine.
We opened our eyes to behold the world
And the bubble burst . . .

9

hūsh ast ki sarmāye śad dard-e sar ast
fārigh-e bāl ānki az jahān bī khabar ast
dar baiżah namī kunand murghān faryād
har chand ki baiżah az qafas tang tar ast

10

barkhīz Ghanī havāye farvardīn ast
may nūsh ki vaqt-e bādah khurdan ast
faślī ast ki āshiyān-e murghān-e chaman
az kaṣrat-e gul chūn sabad-e gulchīn ast

11

bad garchi damī chand ba naikān binishast
sar rishtaye nīkīyash nayaftād ba dast
az tīrah dilī pāk nashud khākistar
har chand ki ba ātash-u-āyīnah nishast

12

bar ghamzadgān ahl-e jahān mīkhandand
az jūsh-e faraĥ ba śad dahān mīkhandand
dar bazm-e ṭarb ba sān-e mīnāye sharāb
mā mīgiryīm u dīgrān mīkhandand

9

Awareness: the source of countless headaches.
Blissful is the man unmindful of the world.
Birds wail not while unhatched,
More confining than a cage though the egg be.

10

Rise, Ghani, for the breeze of spring is here.
Sip wine, for the time of vintage is here.
The season when the nests of garden birds
Resemble the rose gatherer's basket is here.

11

Evil may spend some moments with the virtuous,
Yet virtue's blessings will scarcely touch it.
The company of flame and mirror it might keep,
But can soot rid itself of its blackness?

12

Men scoff at the grief-stricken
And make fun of their misery.
Like the wine flask which entertains revellers,
We shed tears that others may rejoice.

13

tā charkh-e falak chū āsiyā hast bigard
chūn śubĥ na dārīm ghizā juz dam-e sard
mā kāsah na dārīm ki diryūzah kunīm
diryūzah barāye kāsah mībāyad kard

14

chūn dar gham-e Khurshīd fighān bar khīzad
har kas shinvad az dil-u-jān bar khīzad
bar turbat-e ū zi dīdah mī rīzam āb
shāyad ki azīn khwāb-e girān bar khīzad

15

har kas ki ba khwīshtan gumāni dārad
chūn dar nigarī ʿaib-e nihānī dārad
ʿumrīst ki dar bāgh-e jahān gardīm
har mīvah ki dīdam ustukhwānī dārad

16

chūn nīst dar uftādgiyam kas rā shak
bar khāstah az chi rū ba jangam har yak
dāʿvaye barābarī na dāram bā kas
ba khāk chirā barābaram kard falak

13

Like the millstone, heaven's wheels keep turning.
And like dawn, I heave cold sighs for my bread.
Too poor to own a bowl to beg for bread,
It befits that I beg for a bowl instead.

14

Cries of grief rend the air for Khursheed
And raise tumult in the hearts of men.
I, for one, shed tears on his grave
Perchance they wake him up from slumber.[72]

15

O you who are filled with self-conceit,
Pause and look for a blemish within.
Years have I spent wandering the world,
A fruit with no stone I am yet to see.

16

When no one doubts my humility,
Why then have men risen against me?
I claimed to be a match to none,
Yet the heavens have levelled me with dust.

17

mastān hamah khuftah and dar sāyaye tāk
az garmiye khurshīd-e qayāmat bībāk
dunyā gūyand mazra'-e ākhirat ast
ay sheikh birīz dānaye subĥa ba khāk

18

ay dar gham-e nūr-e dīdah chashmat namnāk
Yā'qub ṣifat jāmaye ṣabrat ṣad chāk
dar mātam-e farzand marīz ashk ba khāk
ṣad ṭifl makun barāye yak ṭifl halāk

19

az khalq ba gūshaī nishastam pinhān
mīgardad azīn rāh sukhanam gard-e jahān
tarsam ki digar sukhan shavad gūshah nishīn
az khānah bīrūn āyam agar hamchū zabān

20

tā ghunchah shud az sir-e dahānat āgāh
gardīd zabān-e guftugūyash kūtah
zad lāf zi hamrangiye la'l-e tū nigīn
ākhir ba durūgh rūye khud kard siyāh

17

The drunk are asleep in the vine's shade,
Fearless of doomsday's scorching sun.
Tomorrow, they say, you'll reap what you today sow.
To dust then, O sheikh, let your beads go.

18

O you, whose eyes are grieving for the dear one lost!
Like Yaqub, the mantle of your patience is torn to shreds.
Let not all your pearls be lost to dust.
Squander not a hundred in grief for one.

19

From men I have hidden myself in seclusion.
This way has my verse travelled the world.
I fear my verse might take to seclusion,
If like the tongue I come out from my cavern.

20

Ever since to the bud your mouth's core was unveiled,
Its prattling tongue has greatly shrunk.
As the gem bragged of similitude to you,
Its face was tarnished by the lie it uttered.

21

ay burdah jamāl-e tū khurshīd kulāh
rukhsār-e tū ātash zadah dar khirman-e māh
az khijlat-e rūye ātashīnat Yūsuf
tā āb nashud bīrūn nayāmad az chāh

22

ay bād-e śabā ṭarb fazā mī āyī
gūyā ki zi kūye yār-e mā mī āyī
az kūye ki barkhāstah-ī rāst bigū
bisyār ba chashmam āshna mī āyī

21

O you, whose beauty eclipsed the sun!
Whose radiant cheek set the moon ablaze!
Yusuf, abashed by your refulgent face,
Tarried in the well until drenched with shame.[73]

22

O morning breeze, your arrival enhances my joy.
Perhaps you come from my love's street.
From whose street have you risen, truly speak?
You captivate my eyes with such a fascinating sight!

Winter's Tale

(*Maṣnavī Shitā'iyah*)

darīn mausim az baski yakh bast āb
shud āyīnah khānah sarāye ĥabāb

ba śahn-e gulistān khaṭ-e jūye āb
numāyad ki chūn jadval andar kitāb

daf az dast-e muṭrib nashud āshkār
ki bastah ast yakh-e naghmaye ābdār

chunān kard dar āb sarmā aṣar
ki naqsh bar āb ast naqsh-e ĥajar

hamīn naghmah baṭ mī sarāyad dar āb
'khushā hāl-e murghī ki gardad kabāb'.

chunān āmad ātash zi sarmā ba tang
ki gardīd pinhān dubārah ba sang

zi ham ātash u shu'lah uftād judā
bigīrad agar yak nafas az havā

sharārī gar uftād zi ātash judā
shavad ĵāla dar yak nafas dar havā

shudah khushk az bas zi tāṣir-e bād
zi 'ainak dihad pardaye chashm yād

Winter's Tale

In this season when the water is frozen
Every bubble has become a glasshouse.

The stream flowing across the garden
Looks like a line drawn on the page.

The minstrel's hand is without a drum.
It seems the dewy song has frozen too.

Cold has turned water into ice.
Etching it is like etching a stone.

In all this, the duck in the water croons
'Lucky the bird that's become a kebab.'

The spark too has been struck by the chill
And has hid itself back in the flint.

The spark and flame are together no more.
The chilly draught has torn them apart.

No sooner does a spark rise from the fire
Than it turns into a hailstone.

Such is the nip in the biting air
That the moist eye resembles a stony glass.

chunān mardum az āb dārand bāk
ki nihafta ast āyinah rū ba khāk

buvad barg-e 'ishrat badast-e chinār
ki faśl-e khizān ātash āvardah bār

azān dādah māhī tan-e khud ba khār
ki shāyad bagardad ba ātash duchār

zi bas sard gashtah tannūr-e siphar
na dīdah darū garm kas nān-e mihr

ravān chūn shavad bar zamīn jūye āb
ki bastah ast yakh chashmaye āftāb

zi sarmā damī yāft māhī najāt
ki az tīgh-e yakh kardah qat'-e ĥayāt

zi bas barf rā nīst parvāye āb
ravad chūn kaf-e baĥr bālā-e āb

buvad akhgar az manqal-e ātshīn
namūdār chūn az nigīn dān nigīn

ravad pāyash az takhtaye yakh zi jā
chū khaṭ har ki uftad zi kursī judā

Scared to their bones now men are of water.
Like the mirror they hide it under the earth.

The means of living are in the hands of chinar
Which in autumn has provided for fire.

The fish offers itself to the hook
In the hope that it might see fire.

So cold has the oven of the sky become
No longer visible is the bread-like sun.

Can a stream flow on the face of the earth
When the sun's eye itself is frozen?

Release from the stinging cold does the fish find
When it slits itself with the icicle's sword.

No fear of water does the snow show.
It floats on its surface like foam.

The ember glowing in the brazier
Looks like a gem in the casket.

He who relaxes his hold on the chair
Finds himself skating on the ice.

kasī rā ki dar sang-e yakh pā sikasht
zi kursī barū mītavān takhtah bast

shud afsurdaye dar jahān kāmgār
ki chūn sang-e ātash kashad dar kinār

darīn lāye gil chūn shudī kas ravān
namī būd gar pāye yakh darmiyān

zi bas kard sarmā ba māhi aṣar
bar āvar bār-e khud az jāye tar

ba sūye falak har ki sar dādah āh
shudah barf u uftādah bar khāk-e rāh

zamistān barāyīm chi bāzī kunad
ki az āb āyinah sāzī kunad

agarchi girift ātash andar kinār
nashud garm yak lahźa dast-e chinār

zi sarmā ba marg ānki gardad duchār
darīn faśl dūzakh kunad ikhtiyār

chu ṭiflān qadam sūye maktab zanand
bar avrāq-e yakh mashq-e markab zanand

darīn faśl bāshad kasī hūshyār
ki gulkhan nishīn ast dīvānah vār

And he who breaks his leg on the ice
Is plastered there on the wooden plank.

His joy knows no bounds if a sad soul
Gets hold of a few flint stones.

How could one walk on the murky earth
If it were not covered with planks of ice?

Agonized such is the fish by the chill
It seeks to flee from all that is wet.

Every sigh that soars up to the sky
Becomes a snowflake and falls to the ground.

Behold the game that the winter plays
Fashioning myriad mirrors from water plain.

Though a flame hides within its breast
The leaf of chinar breathes no warmth.

And he whose life leaves him in this chill
Prefers hell to escape the cold.

As children make their way to school
They practise skating on the planks of ice.

He is wise who in this season
Clings to the stove like a madman.

zi bas bast yakh zīn bayān bar zabān
zabānī digar shud nafas dar dahān

azāndam ki sarmā dar āmad ba jūsh
na junbad dahān yak nafas hamchū gūsh

sirishkī ki az dīdah gardad judā
shavad bastah chūn ashk sham' az havā

magar zīn havā shud khabardār mūr
ki dar zindagī bahr-e khud kanad gūr

azīn pas narānam zi sarmā sukhan
ki yakh pāraye shud zabān dar dahan

Tazmīn

Hindūye dīdam ki mast az 'ishq būd
guftamash zīn justjūyat chīst sūd

dar javābam guft ān zunnār dār
nīst dar dastam 'inān-e ikhtiyār

rishtaye dar gardanam afgandah dūst
mī barad har jā ki khwāṭir khwāh-e ūst

Narrating this, my tongue is coated with ice.
My breath, it seems, has frozen to make another tongue.

And when the chill turns chillier still
Like the ear, even the mouth turns still.

The tear which drops from the crying eye
Freezes like the wax dripping down the candle.

All this is known to the wise ant
Which entombs itself when alive.

This winter's tale I can no longer narrate
For the tongue is now an icicle in my mouth.

A Linear Graft

I saw a Hindu drunk with devotion.
'Such striving to what end?' I asked.[74]

In reply said that wearer of the sacred thread:
'The reins of will are not in my hand.

"The Friend has yoked my neck with His thread
And pulls me by it wherever He wills."'

Notes

INTRODUCTION

1. Sirajuddin Ali Khan Arzoo, *Majma'un Nafaa'is* (1752), quoted in Ali Jawad Zaidi, *Divan-e Ghani* (Srinagar: Jammu and Kashmir Academy of Arts, Culture and Languages, 1984; reprint), p. 20.
2. *Tazkirah*s are biographical dictionaries.
3. Shamsur Rahman Faruqi, 'Five (or More) Ways for a Poet to Imitate Other Poets, *or*, Imitation in Sabk-i Hindi', 1998, available online at http://www.columbia.edu/itc/mealac/pritchett/00fwp/srf/srf_imitation_2008.pdf. Also see Kishan Chand Ikhlas (d. 1748 or 1754), *Hamesha Bahar* (1719), ed. Waheed Quraishi (Karachi: Anjuman Taraqqi-e Urdu, 1973).
4. Kalim is the epithet of Prophet Musa (Moses), who enjoyed the privilege of speaking directly to God. Being a shepherd, he used to carry a staff.
5. Tur is the mountain where Musa used to receive instructions from God.
6. Quoted in Shibli Naumani, *Sherul-Ajam*, vol. 3 (Azamgarh: Maarif Press, 1956; reprint), p. 75.
7. Muhammad Tahir Nasrabadi, *Tazkirah-e Nasrabadi*, quoted in Zaidi, *Divan-e Ghani*, p. 20.
8. Muslim, cited in the preface to *Divan-e Ghani*, pp. 55–56.
9. P.N.K. Bamzai, *Cultural and Political History of Kashmir*, vol. 2 (Srinagar: Gulshan Books, 2007; reprint), p. 276.
10. B.N. Parimoo, *The Ascent of Self: A Re-interpretation of the Mystical Poetry of Lalla Ded* (Delhi: Motilal Banarsidass, 1978), p. 76.
11. G.L. Tikku, *Persian Poetry in Kashmir 1339–1846: An Introduction* (Berkeley: University of California Press, 1971), p. 32.

12. An allusion to a verse in the Quran which says that God took a covenant from Adam's progeny saying, 'Am I not your Lord?' to which all replied, 'Yes, indeed.' See the Quran, chapter 7, verse 172.

13. S.R. Faruqi, 'A Stranger in the City: The Poetics of *Sabk-e Hindi*', *The Annual of Urdu Studies* 19, 2004, pp. 1–93.

14. Ibid.

15. Paul Losensky, 'Sa'eb Tabrizi', *Encyclopaedia Iranica*, 2003. Online edition available at http://www.iranica.com.

16. Ibid.

17. E.G. Browne, *A Literary History of Persia*, vol. IV ((New Delhi: Goodword Books, 2002), pp. 265–76.

18. William Wordsworth, *The Prelude* Book II, lines 384–86.

19. Paul Losensky, *Welcoming Fighani: Imitation and Poetic Individuality in the Safavid-Mughal Ghazal* (California: Costa Mesa, 1998), p. 214.

20. S.R. Faruqi, 'Conventions of Love, Love of Conventions: Urdu Love Poetry in the Eighteenth Century', *The Annual of Urdu Studies* 14, 1999, pp. 3–32.

21. William Empson, *Seven Types of Ambiguity* (Harmondsworth: Penguin Books, 1961), p. 19.

22. Shamsur Rahman Faruqi and Frances W. Pritchett, 'Lyric Poetry in Urdu: The Ghazal', *Delos* (3) ¾ (Winter), 1991, pp. 7–12. Available online at http://www.columbia.edu/itc/mealac/pritchett/00fwp/published/txt_lyric_poetry2.html.

THE POEMS

1. *Muhtasib* in the original, translated here as prohibitor, was the official appointed to supervise markets, keep vigil on public morality and prevent vice, including the consumption of wine. *Muhtasib* is also sometimes translated as inspector or censor. Reproaching the *muhtasib* is a common theme in the Persian ghazal. The verse is ironical as the prohibitor's arrival results in something he is to prevent.

2. *Anqa*, translated here as phoenix, is a mythical bird, often used as a symbol for rarity of an exceptional nature.

3. The ascetic is the oft-ridiculed figure in the Persian and Urdu ghazal.

4. Yaqub (Jacob) of Canaan, son of Ishaq (Isaac) was a Jewish prophet and father of Yusuf (Joseph). The story of Yusuf, known for his exemplary beauty, and Zuleikha has been a theme of several classical Persian works and is originally based on the Quranic narrative of the ordeals of Yusuf. According to the Quran, Yusuf, thrown into a well by his stepbrothers, was found by a passing caravan and sold in Egypt where he was purchased by a noble. When he was brought home, the noble's wife fell in love with him and tried to seduce him. Yusuf, however, repelled her advances and became a victim of a conspiracy that resulted in his imprisonment. Yaqub lamented the separation from his son to such an extent that he lost his eyesight. Although the Quran nowhere suggests any reconciliation between Yusuf and the noble's wife, it mentions that she admitted her fault before the authorities. Yusuf, proven innocent, was freed from prison and raised to the position of a powerful minister. Yaqub got his eyesight back only when Yusuf sent him his robe. See the Quran, chapter 12.

5. *Saki* is the wine server or cup-bearer in the Persian ghazal who pours wine into the cup from a gurgling flask.

6. Jesus, according to the Quran and other Islamic sources, was a great prophet who, among many other miracles, was also given the power to breathe life into the dead. The verse alludes to the ancient practice of putting a mirror in front of a dying person to check his breath. It can simultaneously be interpreted to refer to the life-giving miraculous breath of the beloved which left the Messiah dumbstruck to the extent that a mirror had to be placed before him to see if he was alive.

7. Jamshed was a legendary king of Persia who is believed to have invented wine and possessed a cup in which he could behold the whole world.

8. *Nafah*, or musk-bag, which the deer nurtures, becomes its bane as it is often killed for its musk.

9. Amulets are tied around the upper arm to keep away evil influences.

10. Perhaps an allusion to the rampant oppression of the common people by the rulers.

11. Ill luck is often conceived as sleeping and good luck as waking in the Persian ghazal.

12. Since it is impossible to find a feather of the phoenix, to draw a portrait resembling her in some measure is impossible.

13. The beloved, by slaying others and only wounding the lover, has put him to shame. In another reading, the verse can mean: 'As long as I avoided your arrow, I had to hang my head in shame like the bow, which is hung down when it does not hold an arrow.'

14. The moon is a symbol of beauty but is smeared with black spots.

15. Antimony is believed to have a healthy influence on the eyes, improving their vision and beauty.

16. Frenzy or madness, a characteristic trait of the passionate lover of the ghazal, is attributed to Majnun, literally, the frenzied one, who in his love for Laila would wander in the streets and plains chased by stone-throwing urchins.

17. The moth that burns itself upon the candle's flame is the symbol of the self-sacrificing lover. The candle, symbolizing the indifferent beloved, finally regrets its indifference by consuming itself.

18. The abode of the open sky.

19. Kafir, or the infidel, being accustomed to adore idols, is invited to see that the idols of the past continue to be adored in the present.

20. Treasures used to be hidden under the earth. Narrowness of the grave suggests a dreadful afterlife.

21. The sky, a metaphor for fate, is here compared to the oven that gives bread when heated. And to heat itself it burns the speaker's desires instead of firewood.

22. The prohibitor's turban, a symbol of ostentatious piety, weighs upon the head of the speaker like a decanter's stopper which prevents the wine from being poured.

23. Kaaba, the cubic structure in Mecca, is the object of the deepest religious veneration for the Muslim. Wine is very often used as a symbol for passionate devotion as against mere ritualism.

24. The knocker and the crevice usually symbolize the waking eye.

25. The horizon changes colour fast and hence the unpredictability of the firmament, which often changes erratically to the chagrin of men whose destinies are linked to those changes.

26. Like the moth is consumed by the candle, the lover too is consumed

by the beloved, but, paradoxically, both become immortal by dying in love.

27. *Huma*, retained as in the original, is a legendary auspicious bird. It is said that on whoever the *huma* casts its shadow becomes king. The black fortune of the lovers is their ill luck which prevents their union with the beloved. But it is precisely this that they consider their boon like the moth which burns itself on the flame.

28. Candles used to be snuffed out with the sleeve.

29. According to some traditions, the sun of the Day of Judgement will be extremely hot, making it an unbearable time for sinners.

30. Probably an allusion to jars of wine kept underground for long periods of time.

31. The habit of poets to sit in a posture with the head tucked between their knees to reflect long and deep on their verses.

32. The *zahid*, or the ascetic, prides himself on virtuous acts and looks down upon the sinners whose records are blotted with sins. He is asked to desist because dark clouds pour forth the heaviest rains.

33. Pure wine is like the blazing sun as it can dry up the sweat shed in repentance.

34. The verse employs the delightful image of sun and shade. The speaker boasts of his poverty by saying that his only attendant is the sun which, by its motion, spreads and folds the mat of shadow for him.

35. 'Daughter of vine' is the literal translation of *dukhtar-e raz* and stands for wine. The verse exploits the double meaning of the word and simultaneously refers to a maiden hidden behind a veil and wine that is kept away from heat. See the introduction, pp. l–li.

36. The pen will never get to see her, while the letter will have the privilege to be held and read by her.

37. Yusuf was separated from his father Yaqub for a long time during which the latter lost his eyesight in grief. The blackness of the eyes stands for vision and whiteness for blindness. See note no. 4.

38. Mirrors are polished with ash to give them a bright shine.

39. According to the Quran, when Yusuf dispatched his shirt from Egypt, Yaqub, living in Canaan, told his sons that he could smell Yusuf's fragrance. See the Quran, chapter 12, verses 94–96.

40. See note no. 29.
41. Cypress is a symbol of freedom. Firmly grounded in the earth, it reaches a great height and does not depend upon the favours of the sky.
42. See note no. 6.
43. The namaz comprises certain bodily movements such as standing, genuflecting and prostrating.
44. Wild rue is burnt to ward off the evil eye. Ironically, his fortune-star rises only when it burns, much like wild rue.
45. The Prophet Musa (Moses), according to Islamic traditions, was given many miracles to counter the Egyptian Pharaoh, among them the *yad-e baiza*, or the shining hand, which he displayed as a proof of his prophethood.
46. Camphor is applied to the dead when performing their last rites. The shroud usually emits a strong smell of camphor.
47. Wandering ceaselessly in a state of frenzy became Majnun's obsession.
48. Mansur Hallaj (d. 922) is a celebrated Sufi martyr of Islam. As the name Hallaj suggests, he was a carder by profession but invited censure on account of his unorthodox views. To him is attributed the very well-known proclamation *anal haq*, literally, 'I am the Truth', interpreted as meaning 'I am God'. He was charged for blasphemy and executed. Although he has remained a controversial figure in the history of Islam, the Sufis have often interpreted his proclamation as embodying the highest truth of the Islamic concept of *tawhid* or unity. *Zunnar*, translated here as the infidel's thread, is often used as a symbol of plurality and disbelief, while the rosary is taken as a symbol of Islamic faith. In some other contexts, the rosary can be mocked at as a symbol of ostentation or lack of true devotion, and is most commonly associated with the ascetic.
49. Jihad, literally struggle, connotes striving in the cause of the truth. Although it was primarily used to refer to the active struggle against the forces of evil, for the Sufis it almost exclusively meant the struggle against one's desires and other baser human instincts. Holding or arresting the breath was one of the common practices of Sufis.
50. The Quran tells the story of Musa and the Pharaoh's magicians whom

the Pharaoh had promised to reward lavishly if they vanquished Musa at a gathering where all the Egyptians were invited. The magicians displayed their powers by changing their staffs and ropes into snakes. Musa, working under divine guidance, threw his staff to the ground which changed into a serpent, nullifying the magicians' tricks. The magicians recognized that Musa was no mere magician and bowed down in submission. See the Quran, chapter 7, verses 104–46.

51. The ascetic, often ridiculed in the ghazal as a pretentious figure, is here lampooned for committing an act of extreme self-aggrandizement. Killing himself under the burden of a huge dome-shaped turban, often a symbol of self-proclaimed religious piety, is meant to earn the praise of those who themselves partake of hypocrisy and pretension.

52. Old age, which is accompanied by white hair, is compared to the moonlit night.

53. See the introduction, p. lii.

54. See the introduction, pp. l–li.

55. According to some Islamic traditions, Jesus Christ was raised to the heavens alive where he will stay till his second coming just before the Day of Judgement.

56. Instead of the wine cups the prohibitor should smash the cup-shaped grapes and hence facilitate the consumption of wine.

57. The beloved's mouth is sometimes compared to a passage to the next world.

58. Several verses of Ghani describe the process of poetic composition. Even the poet finds it hard to capture a poetic theme or meaning that is fresh and striking.

59. *Peer-e falak*, literally 'the old of the sky', is Saturn, believed to be an inauspicious star in some ancient and medieval cosmologies. It was believed to belong to the seventh sphere and thus to be the farthest from the earth. In some Arabic texts, it is referred to as *sheikh-un-nujoom*, 'the oldest star'.

60. Mansur was taken to the gibbet. See note no. 48.

61. According to the Quran, when the noble's wife tried to seduce Yusuf, he fled from the room. Failing to entice him, she chased him till she

got hold of his shirt from behind and tore it off. The tear in Yusuf's shirt is thus described in this verse as mocking Zuleikha's chastity. See the Quran, chapter 12, verses 23–29.

62. See note no. 37.

63. Yusuf, also remembered as the moon of Canaan by poets, owing to his extraordinary beauty. See note no. 4.

64. See note no. 27.

65. See note no. 44.

66. Khizr, in Islamic folklore, is the prophet who enjoys eternal life but always remains hidden from men's eyes, appearing occasionally to a few to provide guidance in spiritual and temporal matters.

67. See notes no. 4 and 37.

68. The appearance of the crescent marks the beginning of every month of the Islamic calendar. When it appears, especially at the end of the month of Ramadhan, it captures a lot of attention.

69. Probably a reference to the handle of the millstone.

70. Kuhkan, literally mountain digger, is Farhad, the lover of Shirin. According to the ancient legend, Farhad fell in love with Shirin but had a rival in Khusrau, the king of Persia. Khusrau promised to give up his claim to Shirin if Farhad could dig a canal through the mountain Bistun to bring milk to the palace. Farhad, to the amazement of all, achieved this, whereupon Khusrau sent him the false news of Shirin's death. Unable to bear the shock, Farhad killed himself with the adze he had used to dig through the mountain.

71. See previous note.

72. Khursheed is said to have been a dear pupil of Ghani.

73. See note no. 4. This quatrain is addressed to the Prophet Muhammad.

74. *Tazmin*, translated here as 'a linear graft', is the practice of quoting one or more verses of another poet. Technically it is part of the *Masnavi Shitaa'iyah*, although detached from it, and elucidates the omnipotence of the Divine. The last distich is taken from Hafiz of Shiraz.